Writing
bestselling
children's
books

Writing
bestselling
children's books

Once upon a time,
far far away...

52 brilliant ideas for inspiring
young readers

Alexander Gordon Smith

brilliantideas

CAREFUL NOW

This book is full of ideas that will help
you navigate your way past publishers'
slush piles and onto the bookshop
shelves. But it will only help if you also
put in the time and effort. There may
be magic wands and spells to ensure a
happy ending in the books you write
but real life doesn't come with a
guarantee, and we can't be held
responsible if literary success eludes
you. We know you can do it if you put
your mind to it though, so pen at the
ready and best of luck.

Published in 2007 by
The Infinite Ideas Company Limited
36 St Giles
Oxford, OX1 3LD
United Kingdom
www.infideas.com

A CIP catalogue record for this book is available from the British Library.

ISBN 978-1-905940-07-3

Brand and product names are trademarks or registered trademarks of their
respective owners.

Designed and typeset by Baseline Arts Ltd, Oxford
Printed in India

Brilliant ideas

6. **And losing *Just William***...21
We all remember children's books from our youth, but just because we got excited when the Famous Five solved the mystery of Granny's missing knickers, it doesn't mean modern kids will. Stay up to date.

7. **Too many E numbers**...27
Kids are psychic – they can always tell when grown-ups are bored. Getting your story to work is all about finding ideas that make *you* hyperactive with excitement.

8. **The golden years**...31
Everyone would like to be a child again, and now you've got the best excuse ever for being young at heart.

9. **Kidspotting**...35
Working out what's hot and what's not in the playground is essential. Here's how to get the most from watching the kids you know.

10. **Bless you!**...41
If you think of research as sitting in a library sneezing over ancient tomes, then think again. Getting to know the world of your story can be an adventure in its own right.

11. **The Bogeyman cometh**...45
Getting to know what kids like is only half of the challenge – finding out what terrifies them can also make your book a winner.

12. **Getting gross**...49
Many writers have written books for children but worried about upsetting parents. However, there's nothing that appeals to kids more than blood, guts and gore!

Brilliant features

Each chapter of this book is designed to provide you with an inspirational idea that you can read quickly and put into practice straight away.

Throughout you'll find four features that will help you get right to the heart of the idea:

- *Here's an idea for you* Take it on board and give it a go – right here, right now. Get an idea of how well you're doing so far.

- *Try another idea* If this idea looks like a life-changer then there's no time to lose. Try another idea will point you straight to a related tip to enhance and expand on the first.

- *Defining idea* Words of wisdom from masters and mistresses of the art, plus some interesting hangers-on.

- *How did it go?* If at first you do succeed, try to hide your amazement. If, on the other hand, you don't, then this is where you'll find a Q and A that highlights common problems and how to get over them.

Introduction

It's one of life's greatest myths – that writing for children is easier than writing for adults. I mean, short books, no big words, and any gaps can just be filled in with pictures. But nothing could be further from the truth.

Kids are the harshest critics of all. Give most grown-ups a copy of *Ulysses* to read and they'll pretend to like it just so they don't look stupid. But if you give it to kids they'll tell you straight up that it's boring. Writing for children is all about catching their attention and keeping it – whether for five pages or five hundred. And being restricted by theme, vocabulary, length and a wandering attention span makes things infinitely more complicated.

But writing for children is one of the most rewarding activities any writer can experience. To kids, stories are everything – fuelling their imaginations and providing endless hours of entertainment. And more importantly, they help readers find meaning in life, guiding them through the challenges and difficulties of childhood and allowing them to grow. A good children's book will provide inspiration for countless generations, shaping the world as it influences each young mind.

I'd like to say that *Writing Bestselling Children's Books* is a magical tome that will provide the secret formula for creating a masterpiece. But

> **'Sure, it's simple, writing for kids... just as simple as bringing them up.'**
> URSULA LE GUIN

Defining idea...

the truth is that there are no rules to creative writing. It's not like putting up a flat-pack wardrobe or learning to programme your television. But this is a good thing – if there were set rules to follow then all books would be the same, and nothing would be worth reading.

The truth is that all good writing, especially for children, must come from the heart, from the soul, and from your own spirit of fun and adventure. It has to be personal, a piece of you unleashed on the page. The only way children will embrace your story – believe in it so ferociously that it will become part of them – is if you live it. That, in essence, is what makes a good writer.

'The stories of childhood leave an indelible impression, and their author always has a niche in the temple of memory from which the image is never cast out...'
HOWARD PYLE, US writer and illustrator

This book is a collection of the hints, exercises and priceless nuggets of information I've picked up over the years as a writer, editor and publisher – the inspirational ideas I use to write my own children's books. Some of this is centred around the technical details, but what I really hope the book does is help you harness your creative powers, free your inner child and help you become so excited by your own imagination and the characters that live there that writing it down becomes a joy – an adventure in its own right.

It's worth confessing to the fact that I'm the sort of person who buys books on health and piano tuition because I think that the simple act of reading them will give me a six-pack and let me play the *Moonlight Sonata*. Don't take this approach with your writing. While this book will hopefully point you in the right direction, the only way to really be successful is to keep writing. Good luck!

1

In the zone

**'I'm going to write my book as soon as I've the time!'
But if you really want to be successful, you have to make
time and space to write.**

It's easier said than done. What with working, dealing with children, partners who might not understand your ambitions — free time is a commodity that you're not even sure exists any more.

No matter how busy you are, however, it's essential that you devote time and energy to your writing every day. I've known people who always wanted to write, who carried an idea in their heads for years, but because they were so busy all the time it just never happened – their ideas faded, their ambition died and what could have been a wonderful children's book was never written. Don't surrender your stories to limbo – there is always more time in the day than you think.

Here's an idea for you...

It's the most simple, but the most important, thing that any writer must do. Buy a notebook, one small enough to be carried wherever you go. Every time you are inspired with an idea, a character trait, a plot point or an evocative description, write it down. Make yourself a promise – that you'll write something every day, either in your notebook or on your computer. Before you know it you'll be finding time everywhere.

TIME IS MONEY

It may be an irritating statement, but in many ways it's true. Like money, you only have so much time, and you have to know how to spend it for maximum effect. And in the same way as you'd save money if you wanted to buy a new television, you have to learn how to reallocate time from various other areas of your life so that you can afford to spend a little of each day writing.

Take a closer look at how and where you spend your time, focusing on those things that aren't absolutely necessary. Do you watch television or play computer games in the evenings? Do you read the paper while eating your breakfast? Do you get out of bed at the last possible minute, or go to bed earlier than you need to?

A STITCH IN TIME

The chances are you've answered yes to more than one of these questions, which means that you *do* have time to write. Even if you don't actually sit down at a computer during these short breaks, use the time to write notes and thoughts in a notebook. Play with ideas, work on short sketches, character descriptions or snatches of dialogue. These are a great source of inspiration when you do finally sit down to write. Instead of staring at a cold screen thinking you have to start from scratch, your brain will be warmed up and ready to go.

Even during the times that you can't write things down – when you're walking to work, cleaning the windows – keep thinking about whatever you're working on. Picture your characters, imagine your fictional world, unknot any tricky plot points in your head, and write it all down when you get the chance. This thinking time is almost as important as writing itself.

If you really can't work in the chaos of the home then make the most of your time outside. Check out IDEA 5, *Finding Harry...* for some great ways to look for ideas.

Try another idea...

THE HOURS

Snatching bits and pieces of time here and there is great for keeping your passion alive, but if you truly want to be a published author then you have to write for a set amount of time *every day*. Try and give yourself an hour or so which is your own time, a time you can slip into your literary world and just write without distractions, without feeling guilty (make sure it's a time when your mind is at its most alert and creative). Pick a space which is your own, where you feel comfortable and relaxed. Tell friends and family not to disturb you unless the house is on fire, unplug the phone and don't let yourself be sidelined by anything.

Finding this time and space may seem impossible, but there are twenty-four hours in each day and I know you can free up one of them – even if it means getting up an hour earlier each morning or going to bed an hour later. And if you only manage to squeeze in 200 words during each hour, at the end of a year you could have written a 75,000-word book.

'As cows need milking and sweet peas need picking, so writers must continuously exercise their mental muscles by a daily stint.'
JOAN AIKEN

Defining idea...

3

How did it go?

Q   I'm not quite sure what to write in my notebook. Any hints or suggestions?

A   *See your notebook as a net – a way to catch the fleeting thoughts and precious ideas that flutter in the back of your brain. Don't assume that just because you're thinking of something now you'll remember it in an hour's time, or the following morning – the chances are you won't. Write it down so that you don't have to remember it. Get into the habit of doing this every time you see something that has some resonance with your work. The notebook should become a record of your own experience, and the personal interest invested in these scraps will help bring your writing to life.*

Q   My house is a zoo and my computer room is the monkey house. Is there a solution that doesn't involve tranquillising my family?

A   *If you really can't find space, even when the kids are in bed, then try and escape for an hour a day. Find a quiet spot in the garden, even in the shed (luminaries such as Roald Dahl and Philip Pullman have written in the garden shed), or visit the library, a museum, a bookshop or a favourite café. You don't have to be near the computer, just take your notebook and a pen and write the old-fashioned way. It doesn't matter where you are, as long as you have time and space to think.*

2

The uses of enchantment

Writing for children is about more than entertainment. For as long as humans have been around, stories have helped children find meaning in life, and discover their place in the world.

Any successful book will do the same. No pressure.

Stories – whether they are fairy tales or myths or novels – have always been our most fundamental way of understanding who we are, of making sense of our existence. For children especially, who discover so much about life and its inherent struggles, pains, joys and rewards through books, stories are far from just entertainment. They are the magic that allows them to grow.

REALITY BITES

The great stories that have been told for centuries, especially myths and legends and fairy tales, are vital because they answer a basic need in all of us – to find stories which identify our own problems in some form or other, but in which we find hope despite these terrible conflicts. Fairy tales aren't real, but the heroes and villains and monsters and quests they encapsulate *are* real because they represent genuine aspects of a child's life.

Here's an idea for you...

Study as many fairy tales – as well as myths and legends – as you can. Make notes about their structure, their heroes and their quests, the monsters and villains that try to stop the main character's progress, even the landscapes. For each character and place, try to imagine what it might represent for a child, and how a reader might see his own problems, doubts, fears and dreams in the story.

Every child knows what it's like to be Cinderella because all children feel unappreciated at times and want to be special. They have dreamed of being clever and brave enough to scale the beanstalk and outwit the giant in the same way as Jack, gaining independence from their parents and proving that they can survive on their own. Fairy tales always start with something terrible, but through their strength, bravery, kindness, humility and luck the heroes usually triumph. And it is their victory which teaches children that, although life is a struggle and they may feel small and powerless, they have the strength to change things.

STRANGER THAN FICTION

Fairy tales represent the real problems and difficulties that exist in every child's life (and every adult's, too). But they work because they distance readers from their problems through fantasy. They aren't didactic or prescriptive or obvious. If they were, they would be presenting a reader with a fixed answer to a problem or a set way of behaving, and the child would learn nothing but rules.

Instead, they show a hero struggling to defeat a monster, or complete a quest or overcome an archetypal villain because this allows children to recognise their own problems in the story. The tales become puzzles, providing a blueprint of how to cope with personal issues and conflicts. The beauty of it is that kids will go through this process without even knowing it, because what a fairy tale does is free the creative side of the brain, enabling them to find their own solution.

Fairy tales can be the perfect starting point for a book. IDEA 19, *Fairy dust*, shows you how.

Try another idea...

For example, they might subconsciously interpret the dark woods that a character gets lost in as their own confusion and fear. And when the hero finds his way through, a reader may understand that confusion and fear often mean change and excitement, and that bad things often pave the way to good ones. They will learn that all individuals, no matter how old, have the power to achieve their greatest dreams and defeat their most terrible nightmares.

GUIDEBOOKS

But what does this mean for you? Well, if you want to write books that will change children, that will enable them to develop the inner resources that will guide them for the rest of their lives, then you have to understand the way that the most basic and important stories work. If you can present problems and conflicts in the same way, show children facing their deepest fears, confronting their darkest desires and overcoming them using their own strengths, without telling them explicitly how to succeed and survive, then you have the foundation for a book that will last through the ages – a guiding light that will change lives forever.

'Our greatest need and most difficult achievement is to find meaning in our lives.'
BRUNO BETTELHEIM, *The Uses of Enchantment*

Defining idea...

How did
it go?

Q Shouldn't we, as responsible authors, be writing stories that encourage children to be good and well behaved?

A *No! Children don't like to be told what to do, they like to make their own decisions and learn their own lessons. If you write a book that gives them explicit instructions on how to behave, or how to deal with a problem, they won't be learning anything except your rules – that's if they read it, of course, because overly didactic books are usually repulsive to children. You should be encouraging children to think 'Who do I want to be like?'. This way they will hopefully emulate the heroes of your story and be good because they want to be, not because they've been told to be!*

Q I'm making notes about my favourite fairy tales but I can only really think of one way of interpreting each story. Is this wrong?

A *If every story you read seems to have the same subconscious meaning then the chances are that you've got something on your mind you're not facing up to. Fairy tales don't just have this magical power with children, they also help adults – but only if a grown-up admits the emotional conflicts exist. Try to work out why you're reading fairy tales in a certain way, and whether it reflects something that's bothering you – it's the perfect way to see how these stories help children.*

3

Haven't you grown!

Anybody who's bought presents based on what children liked last year knows how quickly tastes change. Working out what age range you're writing for will save problems later.

One of the greatest mistakes people can make is to start writing a book for children with absolutely no idea of what age group they are targeting.

Unlike adults, children constantly grow and evolve. Every year they are fascinated by new things, have developed more advanced ways of looking at the world and have vastly different needs when it comes to the books they read. Of course there is an infinite amount of crossover when it comes to kids' books, but it is essential that you pick your audience before you start writing – or your book risks being lost in the limbo between age groups.

GET INTO GROUPS

Next time you're in a bookshop, take a look at the way they categorise children's books. There will be a section of baby books, for six months to two years. After this there will be the simple picture books for two- to five-year-olds, with a selection of

Here's an idea for you...

Be aware of the different levels of language that children use as they get older. One of the best ways to do this is to try writing several short passages, each designed for a different age group, but with the same theme. Write one that can be read to a very young child, one for an eight-year-old, the next for a twelve-year-old and the last for an older teenager. They should give you an idea of how different a story for one age group is to one written for another.

toy books with novelties such as wheels, pop-ups and so on. Shuffle a bit to your right and you'll find the section for beginner readers – more sophisticated picture books for children aged roughly five to seven who are just starting to read for themselves.

The young fiction range is for six- to eight-year-olds – short chapter books and series books. The mammoth section next to this is known as core fiction, aimed at eight- to twelve-year-olds. Here you'll find the *Harry Potters* and *His Dark Materials*. Tailing on from this is the young adult range for twelve and up. These categories may seem artificial and unnecessary, but publishers tend to use exactly the same age groups.

HOW OLD?

If you're already brimming with ideas for a children's book then sit down and work out exactly what audience you're targeting. You may have an excellent fantasy plot in mind that you want to use in a picture book, but ask yourself honestly if the limited space of this format, and the estimated readership, will really allow you to do your story justice. Likewise, you may want to write a core fiction novel about, say, the lives of some toys in a shop – a theme that might be better suited to a picture book.

If you've only ever thought about writing a 'children's book', and never given much thought to its exact audience, then try asking yourself the following questions. When you think of your book, what do you see – a large, glossy picture book, a novel, or something else entirely? Try imagining your book in another format – does your idea work better when aimed at younger or older readers? Does your book look like another on the market? If so, then what age is that title aimed at?

You should never talk down, no matter what age group you're aiming at. To find out why, check out IDEA 15, *Grow up.*

Try another idea…

How old are the characters in your book? Young children like to read about characters roughly their own age, while children in the eight to ten age group generally like heroes who are a few years older than them. If you're writing a picture book with a teenager as a main character, you may want to reconsider.

This checklist may seem a little basic, but you might be surprised just how much difference there is between age groups. Working out the exact age of your readers now is infinitely less stressful than trying to change a book when it's written – and if you don't feel the need then at least you'll have some rejection slips to dry your eyes with…

'You know your children are growing up when they stop asking you where they came from and refuse to tell you where they're going.'
P. J. O'ROURKE

Defining idea…

11

How did it go?

Q **I'm still not too sure about what age I'm writing for. Should I just start my book and wait and see?**

A *When you're writing for children things can be complicated because you have to think about age and format as well as plot, theme and characters. You need a clear idea of the kind of book you're writing, and for this it's useful to create a short proposal. This isn't an outline for the novel itself, or something you'll be sending to an editor. It's a way for you to get your head around the nature of the book and its audience. Write down the age level you think the book is for, and its genre. Then write the name of your character, briefly describe the conflicts in the book and the character's motivations. This should help you keep your audience firmly in your mind.*

Q **What are the word lengths, roughly for each age group?**

A *There are no specified word lengths (except for series books, which usually have a maximum), but obviously the younger the reader, the fewer the words. Picture books for babies can have as few as ten words, while more sophisticated ones usually have between 300 and 1,500. Beginner readers often prefer simple stories of 500 to 3,500 words, although more confident children could handle up to 10,000. Core fiction is usually around 30,000 words, but Harry Potter has shown that children of that age can happily digest a book with 100,000 words or more. If it's good, anything goes!*

4

Starting off

Writers starting something new can easily feel as daunted as Frodo Baggins embarking on his quest. But overcoming the terror of the blank page is simply a matter of putting pen to paper.

The carte blanche is a writer's worst nightmare because it only exists when you haven't written a single word.

It fights a zero sum game with the author – only one of you can win. And it wages a dirty battle of fear and ridicule, telling you it can never be filled, that your book can never match the great classics of children's literature, that you may as well just give up. But the blank page can be quashed with a simple stroke of your pen.

WAR OF THE WORDS

The worst mistake any writer can make is to try and defeat the blank page straight away with a masterpiece. Putting immense pressure on yourself is an easy way to obliterate your self-confidence and give the blank page a smug victory. Starting a book is one of the hardest aspects of writing, and I hear countless stories of people who have been so determined to go for the big one first time – the ultimate

Here's an idea for you... **If your mind is still blank, then look around your room or out of the window – pick any object and start writing about it. Don't pay too much attention to what you're saying, just keep writing for ten minutes or so, and include as much detail as possible. With any luck you'll find that once you've popped you just can't stop.**

opening sentence – that they end up sitting staring at that blank page for the next ten years (I wish I was joking).

Too many first time writers see the blank page as something sacred – a canvas that they only have one shot at filling. The most important thing to do is to get rid of the idea that you are about to start writing a finished piece of work, or type out a first line of unrivalled genius. Instead, see that blank page as a sandbox, one where you are free to play and build and experiment in the knowledge that if you change your mind, you can simply start again.

DOODLING

Defeat the blank page with a few simple lines or sketches. These don't have to be related to anything you're planning to write – they can just be random words, short sentences, patches of dialogue you heard on your way home from work, even visual doodles of characters and villains. Once you've made that first strike, the power of the blank page lessens.

The key is not to think too hard about what you are writing. Nobody but you will ever see these sketches and doodles, so you've got nothing to feel embarrassed about. Just keep writing and those random words will grow into sentences, then paragraphs and entire pages. With any luck it will be like a dam breaking. Once you've started off you'll find the words come more and more easily, until you segue into your novel or story so seamlessly you don't even know it's happened. And when you get to this stage, the only problem you'll have with the blank page is that there aren't enough of them.

Sometimes the best way to attack the blank page is to describe the world around you. Check out IDEA 5, *Finding Harry...*

Try another idea...

A RUNNING START

If you're still having cold sweats at the thought of facing the blank page then don't panic. Try writing down a few words based on the following suggestions, using these starting points to inspire your own thoughts and feelings and ease you into the creative flow – write about a wedding you went to, the last argument you had, describe a loved one or somebody you fancy. Another interesting exercise is to describe something (an object or trait) you have inherited from a dead relative, and what it means to you.

The most important thing is to try and write every day without fail. Take a blank sheet of paper and write for a set time every morning or afternoon – even if it's just for a few minutes. If you get used to beating the blank page each and every day then you'll soon start to wonder why you were so intimidated by it in the first place. Most of these sketches you'll discard, but others might find their way into novels and stories. Either way, these sessions will help trigger memories, thoughts and inspirations that mean you're never bothered by the blank page again.

'How can one not dream while writing? It is the pen which dreams. The blank page gives the right to dream.'
GASTON BACHELARD, French poet

Defining idea...

Q **I really don't want to spend my time writing about everyday objects – I want to write a book, a masterpiece! Isn't this all a little pointless?**

A *At the risk of sounding like a pretentious git, a book is only a masterpiece when its author has mastered the art of writing well. And that means plenty of practice. Short sessions are designed to develop the creative part of your mind so that it works all the time. If you get used to describing everything and everyone around you then when called to do so in your book you won't ever be stuck for words. You can also keep the best sketches, providing a fantastic supply of detailed observations and character portraits that you can incorporate into a finished piece.*

Q **If I'm on a roll then I can beat the blank page every time, but if I take some time off from writing I'm always terrified that I can't start again. What should I do?**

A *In short, don't ever take time off! You don't have to write for long, a few minutes a day will ensure that you never get out of the habit of putting pen to paper and smiting that blank page monster. One trick is to leave the last paragraph of whatever you're writing about unfinished – it gives you a great place to start the next day.*

5

Finding Harry...

Being successful is all about finding an *original* idea that appeals to children. So don't go searching for your own Harry Potter – good ideas are everywhere, not just at Hogwarts.

Every writer panics about not being able to think of a great idea, desperately hoping to wake up with that all-important seed of inspiration.

The simple truth, however, is that if you're waiting for a flash of pure genius or a fully formed idea to simply pop into your head one morning, you'll be waiting for a long time.

ONLY CONNECT

The trick for finding inspiration is not to look for ideas, but to *recognise* them. The seeds of stories lie absolutely everywhere – practically anything you look at could be the spark for a story if you learn to see it that way. Take the advice of P. L. Travers, the author of *Mary Poppins*, and 'only connect' (a phrase she adopted from E. M.

Here's an idea for you...

Spend a day as a detective – grab your notebook and pen and surrender to curiosity and nosiness. Look at everything as though the world is a crime scene, and nobody is who they say they are. Try to find a surprising story behind a mundane object, or the magical history being concealed by the waitress. Don't try and look for amazing ideas, just relax and have fun with your imagination and the chances are you'll soon discover the seeds of something wonderful.

Forster's *Howard's End*) – that is, see absolutely everything through the mindset of a writer. Even the most mundane objects can take on new significance when you see them in this light, and the more you view the world this way the easier it will become. Soon you'll be jotting down ideas on every street corner.

It's all about training your mind. Look around you, what do you see? A *Yellow Pages* – perhaps there could be an innocuous advert for magical services, or a detective agency that specialises in lost toys. Next time you walk down the street try and find ideas in everything. A post box with a fallen letter beside it – one that the character opens, discovering an invitation to join a cult. A lost balloon trying to find its way back to a child. These snippets may not be enough for a whole book, but they can start the creative process, snowballing until your head is swimming with ideas.

STEAL FROM LIFE

Real life is just as full of drama as the most exciting children's book, so learn to raid newspapers and magazines for ideas. Use your notebook as a scrapbook and paste in anything that you find interesting – headlines, photographs of interesting people, bizarre architecture, stunning scenery, vehicles: anything that you might use in a future work. Mix in descriptions of people you pass in the street. Yesterday I walked past a man with a long beard and a briefcase who was explaining to a woman that 'the truth lies in his blood' – it could have been something from a book!

Don't be afraid to use other books, films and television programmes. Watch adult dramas and think about how they could be translated into a novel for children – episodes of *The X-Files* or *Tales From the Crypt* can be excellent inspiration for novels or even entire series of novels. These days, publishers love to compare a book to something that already exists – it's how editors sell new writers to their directors – so don't be afraid to be inspired. *The Inventors* was described as *Charlie and the Chocolate Factory* meets *The Terminator* and, yes, I was influenced by both.

OPEN YOUR EYES

You might not know just how to use these things yet, but each time you go back to the scrapbook new ideas will present themselves. An article about a celebrity wedding might be the seed that grows into an entire novel, the description of a Caribbean beach might inspire a story about some kids who have an adventure on holiday. Again, it's all about how you look at these ideas – see them through the eyes of a writer and they take on hidden meanings.

If you've had a Eureka moment, but aren't quite sure where to take it, then check out IDEA 33, *The Magnificent Seven*, for some pointers.

Try another idea...

Defining idea...

'And above all, watch with glittering eyes the whole world around you because the greatest secrets are always hidden in the most unlikely places. Those who don't believe in magic will never find it.'
ROALD DAHL

How did it go?

Q   Help! Every single idea I come up with has been used before! Why can't I think of anything original?

A   *Relax! When you're really struggling to find an idea it can seem like a hopeless quest – there are millions of books out there. But take a closer look at these books and you'll see that many resemble each other, using similar plots and characters but made unique by the author's voice and style. Even if your idea isn't original, your own unique way of writing, and your own unique life experience, will make the story yours alone. Write from the inside out and the result will be one of a kind.*

Q   I've been stalking people and studying inanimate objects for hours, and although I've had plenty of strange looks no ideas have sprung to mind. Why isn't it working?

A   *Don't worry. Start off with the looks you're getting – write a story about why somebody would get weird looks. Then work backwards – is this person looking for something? Lost someone? The aim of the exercise isn't necessarily to find a workable idea, but to get your brain used to looking at the world in a way that makes it easier to be inspired. Even if you don't come away with any ideas, the practice of observing and collecting detail will help you give depth to your work when you do start writing.*

6

And losing *Just William*

We all remember children's books from our youth, but just because we got excited when the Famous Five solved the mystery of Granny's missing knickers, it doesn't mean modern kids will. Stay up to date.

There are many classic children's books which will never, ever go into retirement — great adventure stories that have been favourites with adults and children alike for decades, or even centuries.

It may be that one of these has inspired you to become a children's writer, or that you wish you could create a story that will last as long as one of the great canonical children's books. But before you try and write something that you would have loved in your childhood, open your eyes.

Each generation of children is radically different from the last, and if today's kids think that your book is dated they'll get about as excited by it as they do by one of Granddad's rambling war stories. If you ignore the rapidly changing market and

Here's an idea for you... **An exercise that will help you see the difference between the tone and content of a classic and that of a modern book is to take one of your favourite scenes from a classic and rewrite it as though it was appearing in a novel that could be published today. Try and keep the same spirit of adventure, action and excitement but change the language and pace to make it more suitable for today's kids.**

write something modelled on your childhood favourites then you'll never get an audience because publishers will turn it down.

CLASSIC JURASSICS

This isn't to say that you shouldn't read the classics. If you want to write for children then you should have run the gamut when it comes to kids' books – everything from *The Wind in the Willows* to *Treasure Island*, *Millions of Cats* to *Swallows and Amazons*. There are some aspects of storytelling that are timeless, and the classics effortlessly display the combination of exciting language, rich ideas and unforgettable characters that are essential for any good book.

But the fact is that most classics, if presented to a modern publisher, would never make it. They would be branded as unsuitable for the generation of kids that has replaced the one which read them first time around. Part of the problem is the sheer amount of media fighting for a child's attention. With computer games, the internet, thousands of television and radio channels and new films released every week, books have to be breathlessly exciting and fast-paced in order to compete – especially for the eight-plus age group.

TAKE IT...

There is little doubt that most classics have riveting plotlines and adventures that any kid would still want to experience today. Authors such as Enid Blyton, Arthur Ransome, R. L. Stevenson and C. S. Lewis all had a wonderful grasp of what it is to be a child, the things they dream and the games they play. They described the make-believe world of children in such exciting, heady detail that it is impossible not to be drawn into the story (even when, as in the case of Blyton, the writing isn't always at its best).

They also understood the importance of believable young heroes who solved their own problems without the help of adults, encouraging children to think positively about their own capabilities. In short, these authors never forgot the spirit of adventure that everyone has when they are young. And it is this which has enabled their books to stand the test of time.

...OR LEAVE IT

As a children's author you should be inspired by this sense of adventure, and every writer can learn something from the classics about how to really appeal to children. But inevitably many of these books are now dated in terms of content and language, and if you follow the style of your favourite classic too closely then you're not writing for the current market.

Learn more about what things to look for when you read books by taking a gander at IDEA 14, *Stealing beauty*.

Try another idea...

'**When you reread a classic, you do not see more in the book than you did before; you see more in you than there was before.**'
CLIFF FADIMAN, US author

Defining idea...

The trick is to take the essence of a classic and update it for today's children. If you have an idea for a book which resembles a classic in style or content, then think about how the essence of the story, the adventure and the characters, could be made to appeal to a modern audience. This way, you keep the spirit alive whilst ensuring that readers are riveted and publishers make a bob or two – everybody wins!

How did it go?

Q **Well, I've spruced up my favourite classic and I think I might try and get it published. What do you think?**

A *Er... that wasn't really the point. The idea is to help you see what the differences are between classics and modern books, not to try and improve on a classic. It's great that you're pleased with the results, but please don't approach a publisher with the result – if for nothing else than the fact that you might be breaking copyright laws!*

Q **Speaking of copyright laws, what happens if I love a character in a classic so much that I want to write about him myself? Would I have to do it from behind bars?**

A *Hmm... Interesting question! Sometimes characters from classics are brought to life again in sequels or spin-offs. Take* Peter Pan, *for example. This timeless classic has spawned dozens of other books, comics and films such as* Peter Pan in Scarlet, *a novel written as part of a competition to find a sequel. There's nothing wrong with adopting one of your favourite characters, but always check with whoever holds the copyright before you do anything, otherwise a publisher won't touch it. And make sure you stay true to your hero – you won't be the only one who loves him!*

7

Too many E numbers

Kids are psychic – they can always tell when grown-ups are bored. Getting your story to work is all about finding ideas that make *you* hyperactive with excitement.

So, you've come up with an idea about a boy who discovers a stray dog who leads him on a number of poodle-related adventures. Kids will love it. It will be a hit!

That's all very well, but if you have absolutely no interest in our four-legged friends then you're barking up the wrong tree. If you don't feel passionate about your subject, about the adventures your characters have and the world they live in, then your work will have all the vim and energy of, er, a dead dog and any publisher who reads it will instantly want to have, um, a catnap (sorry, ran out of canine analogies).

OVER-EXCITED

When you're going through the process of generating ideas for a story, concentrate on things that excite you. If you think dragons are duller than watching a hamster

Here's an idea for you… **Make a list of ten things that really excite you – hobbies, historical periods, cars, vampires – it could be anything just so long as you really are passionately interested in it. Next, think about a story that could be based on each of the ideas, working out who the main characters could be, what their goals are and who or what stands in their way. Not all your hobbies will have plot potential, but with any luck you'll discover that some inspire great stories.**

hibernate then don't even consider writing about them, even if you're convinced you've got an excellent, original idea. You may think you can write about a subject that doesn't inspire you but, trust me, unless you're truly engaged with the subject, your disinterest will feed through into your writing.

For the moment, just ignore every book that is out there on the shelves – forget the wizards, the teenage spies, the inventors (sorry, thought I'd just throw that one in), and all the other wizards. Ask yourself honestly what subjects truly excite you. Of course, there will be some that are highly unsuitable for a children's book, but look closely at everything else.

PERSONAL TASTE

Start with hobbies. Is there something you've always enjoyed doing that could form the kernel of a children's book? If you've always had an interest in kung fu then you could write about a child prodigy forced to enter a mystical tournament. Even knitting could form the basis of a story – perhaps a character could accidentally crochet a blanket with strange powers. If you're passionate about a sport then write around it – your giddy excitement when it comes to football or skiing will be like a fuel injection for your writing.

Likewise, is there a place or historical period which you've always been incredibly curious about – a location or time in which you've always wanted to live? If you get a shudder of excitement when you think about a dark,

Learn to see the seeds of stories in everything around you in IDEA 5, *Finding Harry*...

Try another idea...

ancient Transylvanian forest or a busy city like Tokyo or life in Ancient Rome then don't ignore it, harness it. It may be a world away from what you were originally planning to write about, but if this is what truly interests you then embrace it.

IT'S CONTAGIOUS!

Don't just think about real things. Ask yourself which books and films you enjoy most, and why. If you get carried away every time you watch *Indiana Jones* or *Night of the Living Dead* or read *Stig of the Dump* then you should be thinking about writing an adventure story set in mysterious locales, or a horror book for children that includes brain-eating zombies or a story about, well, a rubbish tip! I'm not saying copy the idea, but if you capture the essence of whatever

it is you love about these stories in your writing, then there's a great chance that your readers will feel just as blown away by your book when it's published. Excitement is contagious, and if you want kids to feel it when they read then you have to feel it when you write.

'If a child is to keep his inborn sense of wonder, he needs the companionship of at least one adult who can share it, rediscovering with him the joy, excitement and mystery of the world we live in.'
RACHEL CARSON

Defining idea...

29

How did it go?

Q   **None of my ideas have produced any good stories. What am I doing wrong?**

A   *Answer me honestly – are the hobbies and interests you wrote down truly yours? There's no point writing 'football' and 'detectives' just because you think that's the sort of thing you should be interested in. Just forget you're writing a book for a minute and ask yourself what truly excites you. If the answer is 'ducklings' and 'Bavarian waistcoats' then admit it. You'll be able to write a more entertaining and gripping story about a strange subject that fascinates you than a conventional topic you have no interest in. Even the waistcoats.*

Q   **I *really* do have an idea that I think publishers will go for, even though it doesn't interest me one little bit. Can I just use it?**

A   *Well, if you're absolutely desperate to then go ahead (the subject must interest you a little if you're this passionate about it). Better still, try and think about ways to transplant the bones of your story into a plot that revolves around something which excites you. If your idea is a trainee assassin who lives in a fantasy world and kills using magic, but you're really interested in futuristic cities and excellent gadgets, then consider writing about a child genius who uses gadgets to track down and 'sort out' targets. The chances are that you can keep the core of your story but embed it in a world that you love.*

8

The golden years

Everyone would like to be a child again, and now you've got the best excuse ever for being young at heart.

Looking back at the feelings you had when you were a kid is vital if you want your stories to evoke the same emotions. Your childhood makes you the person you are today.

Your history, the sum of your past experiences, is the foundation of who you are. It's what makes you unique. And if you want to write realistically and evocatively then you have to learn to look back at this vast store of memories. Harnessing key moments in your own history can be a great source of inspiration – providing you with a limitless supply of genuine feelings, emotions and story ideas.

EASIER SAID THAN DONE

Of course, if you're like me then there's not much floating around in your brain's memory department other than a nightmare or two and an episode of *He-Man*. I sometimes find it impossible to remember what I was doing a couple of hours ago, let alone decades, and trying to fish for memories from when I was a child produces frighteningly little.

Here's an idea for you...

Think back to the stories that gripped you as a child, those which made you laugh, cry or lie awake trembling all night. Write down snippets of what you remember – images, characters, phrases, events – and try and recapture your emotional response. Learning what made these books so important to you then can help you identify the direction you need to take in your own writing.

The key is to give your fishing trips something specific to look for. Try remembering a few important moments from your past – your first kiss, your first day at school, your first pet, the house you lived in when you were five. With any luck, these prompts will open the floodgates. Think about less specific things – the questions you always asked as a kid, the people you liked or feared, the places you dreamed of going and those you couldn't wait to get away from, the adventures you had in your own back yard.

If you don't think your childhood was exciting enough to write about, then think again. 'Anybody who has survived an average childhood has enough to write about for a dozen years,' claimed Flannery O'Connor, referring to the fact that even a tiny event in a child's life can seem like a moment of great drama, or the end of the world. When recapturing moments from your childhood, don't simply remember what happened – it is vital to think about how they made you feel, about what kind of things motivated you and about how events changed you as a child, moving you inexorably towards adulthood.

DEAR DIARY

Try and capture your feelings and emotions in writing. An interesting way to do this is to create a childhood diary, picking an important event from your past and writing about it as if you were a child again. Try and forget that you are an adult, just relive what it was like to be young, to see – and hear, smell, taste, feel – the world in a completely different way. When you have completed a few entries, try to fictionalise them, building them into a dramatic scene with either a first- or a third-person narrator.

Harnessing memories like this can be the perfect way to add depth to your writing, enabling you to create a vivid picture of your characters and their motivations. The details from these flashbacks can be transplanted from your mind to that of a character, creating a far more convincing illusion of reality. Although your memories may have nothing to do with the plot of the piece you're writing, incorporating memorable sights, smells, tastes, sounds and touches from your own past will convince readers that what they are reading is a genuine experience. Building memories into your writing like this is essential to writing powerfully – it is why something that isn't real can have the strength of something that is.

The memories which hang around longest are of things that scared us. Harness them: read IDEA 11, *The Bogeyman cometh*.

Try another idea...

'**When you write for children, *don't write* for *children*. Write from *the child in you*.**'
CHARLES GHIGNA, American children's poet

Defining idea...

How did it go?

Q   My childhood is full of horrible things that I've repressed, and I've no intention of digging them up. Any other suggestions?

A   *I'm sorry to hear that. But don't ignore any memories, even the ones you might want to stay hidden. Children's fiction is full of dreadful things and villainous characters because we do all have terrifying experiences when we are young. Learn to embrace these memories, see them as a gift, because they will allow you to craft powerful, moving and unique prose.*

Q   I can't really remember much about the books I read as a kid, shall I just read them again now and describe how I feel?

A   *No! You need to capture how books and stories moved you when you were young, and your reactions as an adult reader will be vastly different to those you experienced then. By all means look at the cover to spark your memory, but do your best to think back to what it was about the book that you responded to as a child.*

Q   I do remember things from my past, but I'm not sure if they actually happened. Does this matter?

A   *There's no doubt that you will remember some things completely differently from the way they actually happened, but don't get hung up on this. Remember that you're writing creative fiction, and so as long as an experience or memory feels real to you (even if it's defeating Godzilla) then it will make evocative reading. Emotional truth is what's important.*

9

Kidspotting

Working out what's hot and what's not in the playground is essential. Here's how to get the most from watching the kids you know.

The worst mistake writers can make when starting a children's book is to automatically assume that they know what kids are like.

There's no denying it – children are virtually a different species. They think differently, they act differently and anybody who's tried to follow a conversation between two teenagers knows that they definitely speak differently. If you try and write a children's book without paying close attention to your subject matter then readers will know instantly that you're a fraud.

UNDER COVER

Whether you're writing a picture book or a novel, learning to observe children at every given opportunity is essential to creating realistic characters. Of course, this doesn't mean sitting outside a school playground with a pair of binoculars – you'll be arrested or lynched in minutes. But there are other, less dodgy, ways of observing these strange creatures.

Here's an idea for you...

An interesting exercise that many children's writers use is to sit in a coffee shop or café and write about the children around them. Pick a child who is openly displaying her emotions and describe her. Next, try and write a short story with your own account of why she is upset or happy. Make it as fantastic and surreal as you like, but be sure to include as much descriptive detail as possible.

First, turn to the children you know – either your own, or those of relatives and friends. Pay attention to the way they act when they are around other children and when they are talking to adults, even when they are alone. Make detailed notes about their ages, their interests and their skills, and jot down any interesting snippets of conversation. Never dismiss the games that children play, especially imaginary ones. Try and work out what kind of worlds they are exploring, what roles they are playing, as these fantasies could be the perfect inspiration.

Don't be afraid to ask them what stories they like, what games they enjoy playing, what characters they would most like to be and the sort of adventures they dream about having. First-hand information like this can be utterly invaluable – but, remember, only ask children you know.

RISKY RESEARCH

If you're writing about older children then visit shopping malls or McDonald's at the weekends or get on buses as the schools finish. Pay close attention to the ways that teenagers behave with each other, the verbal and body language they use, the ways that boys and girls behave differently depending on the social group, and write it all down. Much of what you see and hear wouldn't be suitable for a children's book – the language alone wouldn't ever pass censorship, and the extreme cruelty and violence displayed by many teenagers is more suitable for a horror story. Don't try and capture everything word for word, but instead aim to distil the essence of what it is to be young.

For more about looking at the everyday challenges of being a kid, take a look at IDEA 17, *Problem child.*

Try another idea...

WATCH AND LEARN

If you can't observe kids in the real world, and if gangs of teenagers send chills down your spine, then don't panic – there are countless resources out there. Spend time watching children's television and movies to try and gauge what youngsters are into these days, what their interests and concerns are. Buy

'The debt we owe to the play of the imagination is incalculable.'
CARL JUNG

Defining idea...

children's magazines and visit websites designed for children (giving chat rooms a wide berth). Check out toyshops and libraries, watching what kinds of toys, gadgets and books children buy.

Alternatively, try and make contact with a teacher who works with children of the age range you are interested in. Ask about the subjects taught, about those that they show most interest in, what skills they are developing, what books they most enjoy in class. If possible, try and visit a school to remind yourself what the atmosphere is like – the smell, the sounds, the cold corridors.

Whatever you do, don't put off this aspect of research because you think it might be embarrassing – watching kids is vital if you want your book to carry emotional and descriptive depth. If you convince yourself that you know kids when you don't then you'll ultimately pay the price – like lions, children can easily spot an impostor in their midst, and will tear you to pieces. Figuratively speaking, of course, but it will still hurt.

Q Can I use the coffee shop idea when I'm writing about teenagers?

*A Of course, although you might want to change the theme and tone. Pay
close attention to a group of teenage boys, for instance, focusing on the
one who appears to be most isolated. Describe him – noting his body
language, the way he tries to include himself in the activity, his facial
expressions when nobody is watching – and write a short sketch from his
point of view. This can be a great way to give your book descriptive and
emotional depth.*

Q Can't I just work with a kid and let them write the book for me?

A I was lucky enough to be able to write The Inventors *with my eleven-year-
old brother Jamie, and I know for sure that much of its success was down to
working closely with somebody the same age as the book's key
demographic. We spent hours coming up with ideas together, really living
out the adventure, and I had an unparalleled glimpse at exactly what kind
of fantasies and nightmares someone of this age experiences. While you'll
still have to do the writing yourself, employing a young co-writer is an
invaluable way of harnessing the imaginative power of a child. Just
remember to share the credit!*

How did it go?

10

Bless you!

If you think of research as sitting in a library sneezing over ancient tomes, then think again. Getting to know the world of your story can be an adventure in its own right.

It goes without saying that imagination is more important than knowledge, but kids are clever. If you haven't done your homework they're not going to immerse themselves in your imaginative realm.

First, let's put one little myth to bed: that you should only write about what you know. When I was a kid this was drummed into me by an English teacher, who claimed that flights of fancy and action-packed adventures were a waste of time. What she failed to see was that when you are engaged with a story – any story – you *are* writing about what you know because you are emotionally connected to your subject.

BEND THE RULES

Having said that, when you write stories and play games as a kid, there are very few rules – guns never run out of bullets, magical spells have no side effects, space ships

Here's an idea for you... **If you're writing about a character with an unusual or unfamiliar hobby or job, devote a week to finding out everything about it. Then write about what she does and how she feels. Alternatively, spend your week researching an unfamiliar location or historical period, and write sketches from the point of view of the people who live there. This exercise should help you better understand and describe the world of your story.**

don't have to provide millions of kilograms of thrust to escape the pull of earth's gravity. You might think that, as your readers are children, you can get away with the same sloppy treatment of everyday physics. But the chances are that your educated readers will know more about science than you – and if they start to feel that they can't trust the physical mechanics of your story then they might get suspicious of everything else too.

HERE'S YOUR HOMEWORK

Doctor Johnson claimed there were two main types of knowledge – the facts that you already know, and the knowledge of where to find out everything that you don't. So writing what you know means doing your research. Whatever genre you're tackling, from a picture book about a girl who gets lost at a new school to science fiction for teenagers, if you do your homework then you'll be able to make any world seem plausible.

I can hear you sighing at the word homework, but it doesn't have to be arduous. The best way to do your research isn't necessarily to learn everything about your chosen subject, but to immerse yourself in it. When I was writing the *Furnace* books I visited a number of prisons and young offenders' institutes. I talked to inmates and guards, hearing first-hand testimonies about what life was like inside. It was an unnerving and often depressing experience, but it gave me an unparalleled insight into the atmosphere of a prison. If you're writing about a real place – a school, a fire station, a forest, even a shuttle launch pad – then try and visit one and make detailed notes about the experience. It's usually less difficult to organise, and more fun, than you think, and will give your writing a real sense of credibility and depth.

What if you're writing about a fantasy world? Check out IDEA 20, *Living a fantasy*.

Try another idea...

DIGGING THE DIRT

Of course, if you're setting your story on the moon, in Roman times or on the mythical world of Baldenbladder then you can't exactly hop in the car and pay it a visit. But this doesn't mean you're let off the hook. Spend time researching everything about the world of your story. Use the internet – information on anything can be found using a good search engine. Buy or borrow non-fiction books describing the place or time you are writing about. Watch films on related subjects and read other novels or picture books with a similar theme.

Just remember that you're writing a book, not a PhD. You don't have to know how many rivets there are in a prison door – just what it's like to be locked up behind one. If you get a true sense of the world that you're writing about then you'll be able to create a story that transports your reader to a new place and time.

'If you wrote from experience you'd get maybe one book, maybe three poems. Writers write from empathy.'
NIKKI GIOVANNI, US poet

Defining idea...

How did
it go?

Q **I'm lazier than a fat cat on a Sunday afternoon. Do I really have to do all of that to create a believable world?**

A *It's your lucky day. Not all research is external and involves getting off the sofa. Internal research, better known as daydreaming, is also an important part of writing. It is vital to be able to imagine your characters as fully as possible – the way they respond to the world and people around them. And doing this involves simply closing your eyes and imagining your protagonists in as many different situations as possible, trying to picture how the world looks through their eyes. You can and should do this research everywhere, but make sure you always write it down.*

Q **I've spent several days following the paperboy and I think I know everything there is to know about his job (and restraining orders). So why does my writing seem stale and lifeless?**

A *There's always a danger that you'll just create a manual for whatever job you're investigating, or a lifeless guidebook for a location. You should be trying to see this world through the eyes of your characters – select the details which are most important to them. You probably won't use most of this research in your writing, but if you know about a character's world it will help you understand the kind of person they are, as well as enable you to better describe them and their surroundings on the page.*

11

The Bogeyman cometh

Getting to know what kids like is only half of the challenge – finding out what terrifies them can also make your book a winner.

Everybody remembers what it's like to be afraid when you're a child — the nightmare of losing your parents, the utter reality of the monster under your bed.

As parents, these fears can seem groundless and frustrating, but for kids they can be terrifying, often overwhelming. And as scary as it may seem, it's up to you to climb back into your childhood nightmares and reawaken the Bogeyman.

THERE'S A MONSTER IN MY CLOSET!

All children have irrational fears, but these fears are most powerful between the ages of three and eight when they have a growing awareness of their own vulnerability, and of death. As a result, they often feel small and weak in a vast world that is frequently confusing and frightening. Combined with the active imagination of a child, these fears take on an irrational dimension, mutating from

Here's an idea for you...

Take the five worst fears from your own childhood and write them down. Then write five different sketches describing a character who is terrified of each thing. The sketches can be for any age group, and from any perspective, but try to harness what it is about the situation that is so terrifying. Describe the scene, but try and get inside the child's mind. For each sketch, also try and figure out the child's solution, however imaginative it may be.

simple insecurities into nightmare visions of monsters and loss – the tangible symbols in the child's mind for everything that is scary, confusing and dangerous.

These fears are almost always triggered by threats to a child's sense of security. Think back to when you were young and try and recall how you felt about moving house, starting a new school, being left alone at night. Do you remember the panic, the sense of powerlessness?

CHILDHOOD BREAKDOWN

Now try to write down some of your own childhood fears. I'm not trying to make you neurotic – these memories can be a great source of ideas for new stories, and invaluable conflicts to inflict upon your characters. Some of the most powerful children's books utilise these instinctive fears to create drama – just look at how many novels start off with the death of parents or the main character getting lost in a strange place.

No matter what age children you're writing for, you can harness their fears and use them to make your story utterly gripping. If you're writing a picture book for four-year-olds, try introducing a scary spider as a character, or write about a young girl who gets separated from her parents at the zoo. If you're planning a novel for older kids then play on similar fears – a twelve-year-old boy losing his parents and being fostered, or discovering a terrible secret that threatens his life. Teenagers may not be scared of the dark, but they have their own nightmares – being excluded from a group, turned down by somebody they fancy or simply leaving their childhood behind forever.

For ways to turn childhood fears into conflicts and challenges in your book, come out from behind the sofa and brave IDEA 23, *Heroes...* and IDEA 27, *Treat 'em mean.*

Try another idea...

SELF HELP

These are all threats that disrupt a character's sense of security, and they can be the perfect way to kick-start a story into action or simply propel the plot along. If kids recognise their own fears in a text then they will be gripped by the story, empathising with tormented characters and desperately rooting for their success. Maintain the tension by always keeping these fears alive – they may change throughout the book as old threats are defeated and new ones awakened, but never allow a fear to be fully resolved until the end.

Learning to face your fears and overcome them is a vitally important stage of childhood. Shying away from something that scares us gives it strength, while confronting it can often give us control. For this reason, it is also essential that your main characters overcome their fears by themselves. By reading about characters like this, children of all ages can recognise and process their own insecurities, helping them understand that they are not alone and enabling them to survive and thrive. Your characters may have help from adults or friends, but if a grown-up saves them then they will have learned nothing from the experience – and readers will doubt their own ability to look after themselves.

'To conquer fear is the beginning of wisdom.'
BERTRAND RUSSELL

Defining idea...

How did it go?

Q   **I'm fine describing the horrible situations my character's in, but I'm not quite sure what you mean about her 'solution'. Do you just mean run to her parents screaming?**

A   *That's one solution. But I was talking about the ways that children try and cope with fear by using their imaginations. When faced with a threat, kids will often think of weird and wonderful ways of overcoming it. These can be anything from inventing a crazy monster or machine to hunt down the threat and kill it, or using bombs and lasers to destroy any enemies. Others bring in heroes from books, films or video games to help or think of an object that has the power to vacuum, melt, or just vanish the threat. Thinking about the ways that children use their imagination as a safety net can really help you get inside the minds of your characters.*

Q   **I'm trying to think of things I was afraid of as a kid but nothing springs to mind. You couldn't provide a few examples, could you?**

A   *One of the reasons you might be struggling to remember these things is that, as an adult, you've come to rationalise and dismiss them. Don't try and remember specific fears, just attempt to recall what it was like to be afraid – cold sweats, quickening heart rate, nausea, lying awake, headaches. Once these memories return, the fears they were inspired by should flood back.*

12

Getting gross

Many writers have written books for children but worried about upsetting parents. However, there's nothing that appeals to kids more than blood, guts and gore!

Violence isn't something you tend to associate with kids' books, but it has played an important part in children's literature ever since people started telling stories.

Just look back at some of the fairy tales you were told when you were young – the deaths, the imprisonments, the brutality of the villains. Some were scary, some revolting, but they were all undeniably thrilling. Writers like Roald Dahl – the master of the grotesque – have come under severe criticism for translating this violence into their work, albeit in a comic manner. But critics fail to understand that, handled in the right way, this is an essential tool for helping young readers cope with the often dangerous world around them.

Here's an idea for you...

Getting the right balance can be tricky – you don't want to wuss out from the gory details but at the same time you don't want to scar a child for life. When I started writing for kids I took some scenes from my favourite adult horror movies and turned them into very short stories suitable for my eleven-year-old brother. Try that, aiming to keep the sense of danger, tension and terror with none of the gory details.

THE DARK SIDE

Dahl intuitively understood that children need a certain level of danger and cruelty in their stories because they need to make sense, in a symbolic way, of their own feelings of anger, hatred and powerlessness. Like fairy tales, Dahl's work is stuffed full of disgusting events and frightening characters – look at the punishments *The Twits* administer to each other. The violence isn't just there to entertain, but serves the purpose of telling the reader that there are bad things in the world, and that a struggle is an essential part of life.

But, like fairy tales, Dahl's books are essentially complex narratives of wish-fulfilment which teach that although there is violence in the world, it can be overcome. In all of Dahl's stories, children triumph over adults using their own powers and their own ingenuity. For young readers who have their own complex relationships with grown-ups, and who often feel intimidated or restrained by them, there is no more rewarding fantasy.

CARICATURE

Another way of making delightful unpleasantness work in your book is by caricature – a technique that Dahl turned into a fine art. Just look at the 'grizzly old grunion of a grandma' in *George's Marvellous Medicine*, with her 'small puckered-up mouth, like a dog's bottom.' Dahl also knew that caricature wasn't simply describing the most hideous individual imaginable – it was all about seeing things as children do. His characters, as a result, are grotesque extremes, but children find something unmistakably real in the way they look and act.

Violence and caricature in children's books are often linked to our deepest, darkest childhood fears. Check out IDEA 11, *The Bogeyman cometh.*

Try another idea...

GETTING BLOODY

If you are thinking of using violence in your writing, then make sure it's there for the right reasons, and that – like all dangerous things – you handle it with care. Following Dahl's lead and introducing morbid comic violence and caricature into a book will often get laughs on the playground, but it will only make it a good story if you take time to look at the way kids feel about grown-ups, the way they can often be intimidated by them.

Don't simply create a grotesque villain and unleash a series of bad things upon him. Think about a grown-up kids might fear – a teacher, a neighbour, even a parent – about how they might see him, about what they'd like to do with him if they had their own way. Try to recall the people you were wary of as a child, and the way they looked; you often remember these childhood villains as caricatures. Above all, try to understand the feelings of powerlessness and rage that all children sometimes feel towards their elders.

'Part of the reason for the ugliness of adults, in a child's eyes, is that the child is looking upward, and few faces are at their best when seen from below.'
GEORGE ORWELL

Defining idea...

51

More gritty violence can also be used to good effect, especially in horror and fantasy books. Take Darren Shan's excellent *Cirque du Freak* series as an example, which includes decapitations, blood sucking, hands being bitten off, slashings, mashings and lots more besides. Aimed at the ten-to-twelve age range, these books give a great sense of bloodshed without ever going into gory detail – a technique that other writers should follow if they ever want to see their scary books on the shelves.

How did it go?

Q   I'm trying to write a horror scene for kids, but it's turning into a bloodbath. How can I get all of the thrills with none of the kills?

A   *If you can't convey a scene of violence or horror without resorting to startling, graphic imagery, then get the senses and thoughts of your protagonist to do all of the work. Describe it through the emotions and horrified response of your hero. When I was writing* The Inventors *I had a scene where the two heroes witness a friend's parents being chewed up by a robotic dog controlled by the book's villain. I had them close their eyes. 'But that couldn't protect him from the sounds. The awful noises of ripping, tearing and screaming that filled the room...' This allows the reader's mind to fill in the gruesome details.*

Q   What's the best way to visualise a nightmarish figure?

A   *If you're having trouble describing a gruesome character then try drawing him first. Sketch a caricature in your notebook, thinking about how the character would appear to a child and exaggerating your picture to fit. If this doesn't work, find some hideous cartoons of people – like Steve Bell's often terrifying ones in* the Guardian. *Cut out various features that might belong to your character and paste them into your notebook until you've created a unique individual, then describe the awful result in words.*

13

Splitting sides

According to official statistics, children laugh 300 times a day – nearly twenty times more than adults. But, as most kids know, the majority of jokes adults tell are painfully bad.

Follow these tips to ensure that your young readers are rolling in the aisles.

Children love to laugh, and if they find an author who can keep them in stitches then they will keep on reading. Take a look at almost any successful children's book, for practically any age, and you'll see that it embraces humour. Jokes may lie on every page, as in the books of Jeremy Strong or Philip Ardagh, or they may be mixed with horror and action sequences, as with J. K. Rowling, or they may even be few and far between. But one thing is guaranteed – they'll be there somewhere.

I'VE FORGOTTEN THE PUNCHLINE

If you're anything like me, then you're hopeless at telling jokes in public. Either your mind goes completely blank when you try and say something funny or you blurt out something you hope is hilarious but which leads to nothing but an awkward silence.

Here's an idea for you...

Start paying close attention to the things that make you laugh and write them down in your notebook, dividing them into categories – word play, mishaps, toilet humour, etc. Use books and television – for adults and children (note what the differences are) – and think back to incidents that have made you laugh. This can give you a much clearer idea of why things are funny, enabling you to incorporate similar jokes into your writing.

Don't let this bother you – as a writer you have all the time in the world to think of your jokes, so just sit back, smile and let the good times come. The key to successful humour is remembering what you laughed at when you were a child, and not just jokes but events, things people said, the way they behaved. When I was about eight my dad (who was quite a stern man at times) had a go on an aerial slide that went across a lake. He'd been telling us all day not to get wet, but he sat on the wrong part of the slide and ended up waist deep in water. I still don't think I've ever laughed so much. Recalling incidents like that will give you a great starting point for comedy because you can put characters in similar situations.

Related to this is a cardinal no-no – don't write about the things that you and other adults find funny about children. Kids can be hilarious at times, intentionally and not, but often only grown-ups laugh. Incorporating these elements into a book will make young readers feel like you're laughing *at* them.

DISRESPECTING YOUR ELDERS

One of the things that almost always makes children laugh is seeing adults mess up. Like my dad's mishap, grown-ups who get things wrong or say things incorrectly can be hilarious, especially when they're trying to be serious. Undermining a character like this, especially when it benefits a young protagonist, can be a great way to get your readers rolling in the aisles – so long as it isn't overused (if there's one rule, it's that too much of the same thing always becomes boring, especially for older readers).

This form of humour also helps bolster the relationship between you and your audience – you're on their side, and you're giving them a sense of empowerment over their elders. Another way of achieving this effect is to give kids opportunities to recognise things that are wrong – for example, characters who muddle words and their meanings, and who can be corrected by those reading the book as soon as they've finished giggling.

WORDS AND WIND

Other techniques that can have hilarious results if used well include invented words, especially when used as expletives. Terms like 'oh, piddleducks' can be used as safe swear words and can be great fun to think up. Tongue-twisting names, nonsense words and puns are also potential techniques to bear in mind.

Of course, don't forget toilet humour. Whether you're writing a picture book, a comic novel or even a serious piece with the occasional joke, puerile comedy will always get an audience laughing. So don't shy away from such jokes because you're afraid of upsetting parents. And yes, children like toilet humour, but not all the time – so, once again, don't overdo it.

Learn to harness the funny moments from your own childhood by laughing your way over to IDEA 8, *The golden years.*

Try another idea...

'Cut out all those exclamation marks. An exclamation mark is like laughing at your own joke.'
F. SCOTT FITZGERALD

Defining idea...

How did it go? **Q** **I'm writing a serious book for young adults, and I really think that humour will lower the tone. Can I move on?**

A *Whoa! Even if you're writing a serious book, one with horror and tragedy on every page, humour can be very useful. Used sparingly, it can help lower the tension before or after a dramatic event, helping readers empathise with the characters and immerse themselves more fully into the story. And remember, a single joke in a tragic book can be more powerful than a hundred jokes in a comedy.*

Q **I've been making notes about what I find funny, and have been trying to incorporate these elements into the main characters in my novel. But it's not working... why?**

A *If you're making your main characters the butt of all your jokes then you're making a mistake. Readers see the book through the eyes of a protagonist, and so may see any jokes directed at the main characters as being directed at them. It's fine to make your heroes flawed – in fact, it's essential – so feel free to give them some comedy moments. But reserve the undermining humour for secondary characters. Try introducing a comedic sidekick.*

Q **I've collected plenty of material, should I use it all?**

A *No! The most important rule for using comedy is to be a ruthless editor. If a joke doesn't work, don't use it.*

14

Stealing beauty

Ask authors for their number one piece of advice for anybody wanting to write for children and they'll all say three words: 'Read. Read. Read.'

Of course, this doesn't mean 'Steal. Steal. Steal' — but there's nothing to stop you being inspired...

It's the oldest fact in the book – the more you read the better you write – but you'd be surprised how many people bypass other books and just sit down to write their own. If you leave the books on the shelves you may as well leave your pens in their drawers.

'Every successful writer I know is a great reader,' claims American children's author Robert Cormier. Like most great writers, he learned his craft in the most natural manner possible, lost in a good book. The point of reading isn't to steal ideas, characters and settings from other writers, but to immerse yourself in the world of children's writing, to appreciate just how many incredible stories there are and understand how they're told.

Pick a passage from a book which makes you laugh or cry or feel thrilled and try and imitate the effect in a short sketch of your own. Note what it is about the language used, the description of the characters and the action, and attempt to recreate the effect in your own words. You will probably never use the result in a finished piece of writing, but it can be a great way of improving your technique.

GETTING THE PICTURE

Reading is especially important when it comes to picture books, purely to get an idea of what is out there, and what is publishable. Try and get your hands on as many different ones as possible. Raid the bookshelves of any kids you know, or visit the library. Bookshops are obviously the best place to browse what's on offer. Picture books are expensive, but they're short enough for you to read several while standing inconspicuously in the children's section.

Shops are great places to read books for a number of reasons – you can see which books kids and parents home in on when they're shopping, and can eavesdrop on their reactions. If you're feeling brave enough then talk to the staff, ask them which books are popular and which they recommend to readers. Ask the same questions of a librarian. When you know what the favourites and bestsellers are, read them.

ANALYSE THIS

Try to analyse the books that you pick up. Check to see how many words are on each page, how important each one is to the subject, what their relationship is to the pictures, what fonts and sizes are used. Look at the different subjects and see what they have in common, and try and think of similar subjects that would make an equally satisfying book.

Learn the dos and don'ts of being inspired by the great classics of children's fiction in IDEA 6, *And losing* Just William.

Try another idea...

One of the best ways to read picture books is out loud – even if it is to yourself (you might want to leave the shop first). This is how these books are meant to be read, and it will give you an excellent idea of the rhythm of the text, and the way that the story flows. Don't overdo your analysis – remember that books aren't written to be picked apart – but do study the construction of the text. Try to imagine what the story would be like with a different character, or an alternative ending – and even have a go at writing the same story with different events or themes. It's perfect practice for when you start writing your own books.

I'LL TAKE THAT

T. S. Eliot famously said that 'Mediocre writers borrow; great writers steal'. Obviously this doesn't mean writing a book about a young wizard called Harry, but it does mean that when you read novels there's nothing to stop you being inspired by the characters and their actions – in the same way that you might note down a mannerism from your neighbour, a colloquialism from a friend.

'Reading is a means of thinking with another person's mind; it forces you to stretch your own.'
CHARLES SCRIBNER, JR, publisher

Defining idea...

More generally, look out for your emotional response to a passage. Ask yourself why you're reacting to it and think about ways you can achieve the same effect in your own writing. By spending as much time as you can in the imaginary worlds of other authors, you can inhabit your own with greater confidence. To finish, in the words of Roald Dahl,

'So please, oh please, we beg, we pray,
Go throw your TV set away,
And in its place you can install
A lovely bookshelf on the wall.'

Q   Should I be reading modern books or classics?

A   *Both! Don't limit your reading – try anything and everything and keep your habits as diverse as possible. Remember, though, that trying to write in the style of the books which were classics when you were young won't help you get published. By all means be inspired by those books, but always keep your own writing fresh by reading as many up-to-date ones as possible.*

Q   And just kids' books, right?

A   *Wrong! Read everything!*

Q   I'm producing a carbon copy of the book I'm reading. Can you help before the author comes over and accuses me of plagiarism?!

A   *The idea of the imitation exercise isn't to use the same characters, scene or even events as the original, but to find the essence of whatever it is about the writing that appeals to your emotions, that makes you laugh or cry or want to whoop with excitement. Try using your own characters in your own setting, but aim to emulate the pace and tone and depth of the piece you're working with. If the result doesn't have the same effect as the original passage then try to find out what it's missing.*

How did it go?

15

Grow up

Nothing irritates children of any age more than an adult who talks to them like a baby – even babies hate it.

Just because you're writing for kids doesn't mean that you should write like one. Treat your readers like mature individuals and they'll keep coming back for more.

'Children are always reaching,' said Walt Disney, hinting that no matter what age they are, children like to be thought of as intelligent, thoughtful people who should be treated with respect (even if they don't consciously acknowledge this). If you talk down to your readers – writing in a way that assumes they are idiots – then they won't be your readers for long.

BAD LANGUAGE

Obviously there is a big difference between the level of language you can use in a children's book and that you can use in adult fiction. You're not going to want to use words like 'antidisestablishmentarianism' in a picture book for six-year-olds, but

Here's an idea for you... **Think of a moral or a lesson that you feel is important for children – not talking to strangers, perhaps, or not bullying. First, think of a short storyline that could be used to emphasise this point without moralising or didacticism; it doesn't have to be a complete story, just a short sequence of events. Next, write the scene in a way that makes the message clear but not overt, so that readers can decide for themselves the implications of a character's actions, and not have the message shoved in their face.**

never be shy of using words that you think your readers might not immediately understand – after all, how else are children going to learn new words unless they read them?

Of course, don't start a book with a long list of unusual words – you don't want to make your readers feel like they're not clever enough to read it – but use them when the context makes it clear what they mean. If you've already made it clear that a villain cannot be killed, for example, then there's no harm using the word 'invincible' later in the story. Children love colourful words, and those that they haven't heard before, because it gives them the satisfaction of either learning a new term or guessing what it means.

KEEP IT SIMPLE

Having said this, never try and show off either. Remember that with children's books the role of the writing isn't to show how literary you are, but to convey the story. Almost anything worth saying can be said in short, simple words – and if you keep your sentences tight and your words easily digestible then the book will have greater pace and make more of an impact. Also, because children tend to be slower, more careful readers, if your sentences are too long then they might lose their way in them. Reading your sentences aloud is a great way to check how snappy they are.

The way you talk to your readers is all part of your writing style. Get to grips with this in IDEA 16, *Going out in style*.

Try another idea...

There are sure-fire ways to spot whether you are talking down to your reader. If you've referred to a child as 'little', or any similarly derogative term, then you're also describing the reader that way. The same goes for calling your protagonists 'kids' or 'young ones' or claiming that they are too young to understand things. The golden rule for writing for children is to forget that you're writing for children, because you'll get so hung up on the language you're using that you'll forget about the story. Just have fun, keep it natural, and don't be afraid to experiment.

LESSON OF THE DAY

Another thing that will make kids drop your book quicker than a pile of maths homework is if you're trying to teach a moral lesson or impart wisdom in an openly didactic way. It's absolutely fine for there to be a moral or an environmental message or a lesson about drug abuse at the core of your work, but kids can spot a lecture from a mile away and it's the last thing they want from a book. Build your moral into the story through the actions of your characters, but make sure they don't act a certain way just to pass on your lesson. Better still, just write and forget about the moral – a good story with a believable cast will always teach children in a way that is fun, exciting, and invisible.

'A kid is a guy I never wrote down to. He's interested in what I say if I make it interesting.'
DOCTOR SEUSS

Defining idea...

67

How did
it go?

Q   Holy crap, is it okay to have swearing in my bloody book?

A   *Swearing is part of everyday language – we all use the odd curse, and if you've ever overheard a group of teenagers then you'll know that kids swear more than most. Many publishers are wary of a manuscript that contains gratuitous amounts of swearing, but if you've incorporated the odd mild expletive into dialogue in your book to make a character more realistic then it's usually fine – providing the book is aimed at the twelve-plus age group. If you want characters in a book for younger readers to 'swear' then invent a safe, funny word that can act as a substitute.*

Q   I'm writing for teenagers and my subjects include sex and drugs. I'm trying to curb teenage delinquency, so should I just show the terrible things that happen because of irresponsible behaviour?

A   *The only answer to this question is no. If you write a book where teenage characters just suffer because of their decisions it will be depressing, unrealistic and tiresome. It's fine to show characters making dangerous or irresponsible choices, we all did at that age, but you have to let your protagonists work through their problems and learn from them. Only this way will readers feel that they can learn something, rather than assume they're just being told how to behave.*

16

Going out in style

Just like the style of clothes you wear when you're heading out on the town, the style you choose to write in can say a great deal about you.

Always remember to be confident but not a show-off — just be natural!

If you want to write persuasively, then your style – basically your choice of words – should be personal and unique to you. When you're writing, you have the ability to say the same things a million different ways, so make sure you stay true to yourself.

PERSONAL STYLE

You'll already have a number of different styles – just think about how you write for different audiences. If you were writing a letter to the taxman then you would probably use a formal style with immaculate grammar and words designed to impress. If you're used to writing for adults then you probably employ a literary style, with a more sophisticated register than you'd use in everyday life. If you're sending an email to a friend you're probably writing in a way that's closest to your style of speech, which best reflects your personality – but also one full of shorthand and slang.

You'll develop another style when writing your children's book, and if you want it to be a joy to read, rather than a chore, then always remember that what you're trying to do is *communicate*. Children won't be impressed if you attempt to be clever

Here's an idea for you... **A good way of seeing your style from a fresh perspective is to read your work aloud. Listen for any discomfort in the language, any words that sound artificial, which jerk your attention from the story itself to its construction. Listen to the shape of your writing, how well it rolls off the tongue, how smooth it is. If there are any rough patches, this will help you hammer them out.**

with your writing, if you use ponderous prose and obscure words to demonstrate how well you have mastered the language. Adults may be prepared to wade through tortuous sentences that don't lead anywhere, but children aren't.

EXPRESS YOURSELF

Your style shouldn't be designed to *impress*, you want it to be invisible so readers will be thinking about your story, not your use of words – in other words it should *express*. So keep your language simple, say what you want to say as succinctly and as clearly as you can. Keep your sentences short and punchy, not tangled up in subordinate clauses. If a sentence is getting too long, then make a clause into a new sentence – it will be much easier to read and sound far snappier.

This doesn't mean your style has to be boring or colourless – just remember Shakespeare's comment that 'Brevity is the soul of wit'. Short, colourful descriptions can capture a scene with more life than half a page of detailed, Polonius-style waffling, and an action scene with plenty of lucid, staccato sentences will thunder along with far more momentum than lengthy paragraphs that try and capture everything in a literary style. Powerful writing uses the living, breathing language of everyday speech, and if you use language you're comfortable with then your readers will be comfortable too.

BAD BOYS

Just a few words about the troublemakers – the things that infiltrate your language and scupper your style. For a start, watch out for redundant words – 'she crossed to the other side of the road' is just a clumsier version of 'she crossed the road'.

And beware of adjectives – these descriptive words may look like a shortcut to creating a scene but they are less effective than they appear. If you open a book with 'Adam was a tall, dark, well-dressed boy' then you're not really saying anything. How tall is tall? Is his skin dark or just his hair? And what qualifies being well dressed? Often, adjectives just create a vague image of a person or thing so only use them sparsely, and only when they really say something.

The same goes for adverbs. Don't be lazy and write 'she ran quickly', write 'she dashed' or 'she sprinted'. It creates a much more powerful sense of movement and motive. Last, but not least, avoid using abstract terms like 'love', 'hate' and 'anger'. These are empty and meaningless. If someone is in love, show the way they feel. If somebody is angry, describe their emotions.

You should always keep your style as natural as possible, but it will change depending on the age group you're writing for. Check out IDEA 15, *Grow up*, for some pointers.

Try another idea...

'A good style should show no sign of effort. What is written should seem like a happy accident.'
W. SOMERSET MAUGHAM

Defining idea...

71

Q I've read through my work and every other word is an adjective or an adverb. Should I scrap it and start again?

A *No. Take it and strike through every adjective and adverb with a pencil. Then read it through again, and erase the lines from any words that actually contribute to the text rather than confuse it, the ones you actually need. For the adverbs, try and think of verbs which do the same job – 'he said quietly' could be 'he whispered'. Try writing a short scene without any adverbs and only one well-placed adjective.*

Q I'm writing in the language of the hood, man, and that's solid, right?

A *Pardon me? As a children's writer you want your style to reflect the language and attitudes that exist among young people today (unless you're writing a historical or fantasy piece, of course). But slang words and cool idioms come and go, and if you don't want your book to seem dated two years down the road then it might be best to use them sparingly.*

Q Is it OK for me to copy another writer's style?

A *By all means be inspired by writers you admire; experimenting with different styles is a great way to learn. Ultimately you want your work to be your own, not lost in someone else's shadow, so if you're struggling to emulate another author's style then give up and write in a way that's true to you.*

17

Problem child

Life isn't always easy for children. Problems and challenges lie everywhere – from a new baby to moving house, from unattainable longings to bullying at school...

Understanding these worries is the key to writing a book that will genuinely help, as well as entertain, a child.

For most of us, memories of childhood are seen through rose-tinted glasses – no work and all play and not a problem in sight. But when you're actually immersed in the process of being young things are never that easy.

When you spend a lot of time around children of any age you quickly realise that they have a huge number of worries and deal with a great many problems. These minor issues – from concern about schoolwork to the death of a hamster – may not seem important from the viewpoint of an adult, but inside the head of a child they can become overwhelming.

Here's an idea for you...

Create two characters – one who is six, the other sixteen. Spend time fleshing them out, creating their family, their world, etc. Next, try and think about what realistic problems they might encounter based on what you know about their lives and their relationships, and ways they might try and solve them. Generating characters that later develop problems is a far better way of writing than thinking of a problem and moulding an artificial character to fit.

BAD MEMORIES

The best way to get inside children's heads and work out what bothers them is to think back and dig up all those repressed memories from your own childhood. It may sound a little too much like psychotherapy, but rooting around in your subconscious for those moments in your youth when you were faced with a seemingly insurmountable problem can provide great inspiration for a character. Bad memories often hang around just as long as good ones because they let you remember that you were able to confront a problem and deal with it.

TAKE YOUR PICK

Problems come in all shapes and sizes, and vary tremendously between different ages. For younger children they can include jealousy of a new baby, losing a parent through divorce, not feeling loved, going to a new school, moving house. For pre-teens worries tend to be more abstract, often involving things they want to do, or want to be, but can't – anything from having a new pair of trainers to a desire to be an astronaut. Teenagers have the most complex set of problems, which include peer pressure, sexual feelings and depression.

SLICE OF LIFE

If you're planning to write a slice-of-life book then whichever problem you pick will most likely be the central conflict of your story. But the danger of picking a problem and trying to write a character around it is that this conflict can seem staged, and a character's responses artificial. Any child who is in the same situation as your character will, most probably, know about the problem far more intimately than you, and might find your description of it unrealistic, boring or, much worse, preachy.

The secret to a good problem story is characterisation. Just take a look at books by Jacqueline Wilson and Judy Blume, and the responses they generate from readers. They both write about difficult subjects – from the death of a pet to parental abuse – but they do so using characters that are utterly believable. The important thing to remember is that children are just as capable as – perhaps *more* capable than – adults in using their imagination to solve problems, work through puzzles and find solutions. In fiction, they do not always overcome their problems, but they should always learn to handle them through their own intelligence, willpower and inner strength.

How do you turn problems into conflicts that can drive a story forwards? Learn how to be a real bastard by reading IDEA 27, *Treat 'em mean.*

 Try another idea...

'**A writer doesn't solve problems, he allows them to emerge.**'
FRIEDRICH DÜRRENMATT, Swiss author

Defining idea...

DEAL WITH IT

You should always know your characters intimately before they encounter their problems. If you spend time learning everything about their lives before the conflict begins (before the death of a parent or the beginning of a drug addiction) then you will know exactly how they'll act when the problem arises. If you only know a character through a problem then the response to it will most likely be shallow and predictable.

If you feel strongly about your characters before the problem arises, then when it does they'll react to it in a genuine, heartfelt way, and the thought processes they use to deal with the situation will be unique and therefore realistic. Only when this happens will your book be genuinely entertaining and original, as well as provide hope.

Q **I had problems when I was a child and I handled them fine. Should I just instruct readers on the best way to deal with their issues?**

How did it go?

A *Definitely not! If you're overly instructive in your writing, telling children that this is how they should deal with a problem, then you're not helping. Show them that by confronting a challenge, by handling it in their own way, they can overcome it.*

Q **I'm writing a plot-driven novel so the only problems my characters face are the brain-eating aliens that have invaded their school. They don't need to have 'proper' problems, do they?**

A *Well, if you're writing a plot-driven novel then the main source of conflict will be an external one, and if you give your characters serious slice-of-life problems too it might seem a little too much. However, they will have had lives before the invasion – complete with everyday problems such as family arguments or bullying. If you reference these, even subtly, then you make your characters real.*

Q **My characters are so well developed that they no longer face the problems I wanted them to, and the plot's ruined. What now?**

A *This is a good thing! Listen to your characters and they'll present you with new problems and a new plot, and your writing will be a hundred times more powerful because their worries and actions will be utterly realistic.*

18

Animal crackers

Some of the most successful children's authors have ridden to fame and fortune on the backs of a menagerie of creatures. Here's how to break in your animals and avoid a stampede.

Think back to some of your favourite literary characters when you were a kid and I'll bet you anything that a few had more than two legs.

Some of the greatest children's books ever written have used animals as their protagonists – *Black Beauty*, *Charlotte's Web*, *Watership Down*, *The Sheep-Pig* and *The Tales of Beatrix Potter* to name just a few.

But working with animals can be a risky move. Anthropomorphism – giving animals human thoughts and emotions – is an extremely difficult thing to do well and getting inside the head of an animal will stretch your imagination to its limits. On top of this, modern publishers are extremely wary of books with animals as their main characters. But don't let that put you off – if you hit the right note you could write a book that stays in the hearts of its readers for decades.

Here's an idea for you...

Pick a wild animal, either something you have wanted to write about for a while or something that interests you, and spend some time researching its lifestyle (use books and the internet if you don't want to get muddy). When you feel you know enough, start writing sketches about incidents in the animal's life, giving it human thoughts and emotions but preserving its animal nature.

CREATURE FEATURE

If you want to let animals do the talking, then there are a number of important things to remember. The first, and most important, is don't simply 'dress' humans in animal skins, especially in longer pieces of fiction. The exception is the five-to-seven age range, where you can occasionally get away with having animals that wear clothes, use phones and drive cars.

Little children find it easy to identify with animals – especially cheeky monkeys like Margret and H. A. Rey's *Curious George* who can get away with all kinds of mischief – and editors appreciate the fact that animals don't carry the same connotations of class, race or colour as human characters, making it easier to sell co-editions in other countries. You're always going to have more success with a picture book if the animal characters are animals being animals, not humans in disguise.

DOWN ON THE FARM

This isn't to say that animals shouldn't have human thoughts, emotions and speech – it would be almost impossible to write an animal-based book without some kind of anthropomorphism. Before you start writing, however, it's paramount to set some ground rules. If you're creating a fantasy world, like Narnia, then your animals might be able to communicate directly with people (and this only really works in fantasy). Or, as in *Charlotte's Web*, different species of animal may be able to talk to each other but not to humans. Be consistent, though.

Another thing to always remember is that animal characters work best when they retain their animal characteristics. Before Richard Adams wrote *Watership Down* he spent months researching the way that rabbits behave in the wild, noting their movements, patterns and social interaction. Although he gave his characters human thoughts, and allowed them to speak to one another, they retained the physical attributes and instincts of their real-life wild counterparts. Each character also had a unique, developed personality. It is this powerful combination of fantasy and reality that makes the book so gripping.

CRUELTY TO ANIMALS

One difficulty faced by writers taking on four-legged protagonists is that the dangers and challenges that the hero faces are inherently different to those encountered by a human. Ensure that when you plan your book, you present realistic goals for whatever creature you have chosen, even if they can sometimes prove unsettling. In Henry Williamson's unforgettable *Tarka the Otter* the main character behaves like the wild animal he is, at one point even killing a swan so that he can eat.

Even when you're writing about animals it's essential that each character has a unique personality. Learn more about developing them in IDEA 23, Heroes...

Try another idea...

'It's funny how dogs and cats know the insides of folks better than other folks do, isn't it?'
ELEANOR H. PORTER, *Pollyanna*

Defining idea...

81

In many ways the challenges faced by animals are the same as those faced by children, and you can ensure your book packs a punch by careful selection. Children are terrified of losing their family, of being alone, of getting lost and even of growing up – things that all animals encounter. If your readers can empathise with your protagonist and be caught up in the danger, then they will be hooked. Be true to the animal you are writing about. If you trivialise your characters just because they're not human then you're insulting the animal, and the reader.

Q   **My animal is simply the pet of a main character and these techniques aren't really working for me. Can I ignore them?**

How did it go?

A   *If you're including an animal as a pet – think Timmy the dog in* The Famous Five *– then you will still benefit from giving it certain human characteristics. Although it may not talk, an animal of this nature can be strongly characterised, and should have a distinct personality which can be modelled on human motives and thoughts. This helps keep the animal three-dimensional, rather than simply a prop. Try looking at certain situations from the pet's point of view.*

Q   **I'm using these techniques to bring life to inanimate objects, is that OK?**

A   *Don't ask me, ask publishers – and be prepared for a frosty response. Most editors despise stories where inanimate objects display human thoughts and motives – think Freddie the Fork who went on a quest to find Nathan the Knife. Of course, technically speaking, characters like Paddington Bear and the Tin Mouse from the wonderful* The Mouse and His Child *are inanimate objects with lives of their own, and I even brought a horse-shaped hedge to life in one story. But the difference is that they are recognisable as creatures with unique, developed personalities. Unless you've got a really good idea, stick to humans and animals.*

19

Fairy dust

Fairy tales may have been around for a while but there's a good reason why they've never become boring – these are the purest kind of tales and kids love them.

If you want to tell an adventure story but aren't quite sure where to start then take a look at the oldest stories in the book — the fairy tales.

They are familiar to every single reader, bar none, because they are told in different variations in every country and every culture around the world. They are stories distilled to their very essence, tales that appeal to our darkest desires, deepest fears and most powerful ambitions. And because they are so pure, it's relatively easy to unlock their secrets – anybody can write a good fairy tale!

STORYNAPPING

But before you start writing the story of a poor girl who lives with her wicked stepsisters and who, thanks to a fairy godmother, gets to go to the ball, think carefully about what you're trying to achieve. Your goal shouldn't simply be to write

Here's an idea for you... **Pick your favourite fairy tale and think about how it could be modernised and extended into a novel. Which elements of the story would remain the same, and which would change to make the story 'believable' and exciting to modern readers? You don't have to set the story in the modern world – try a specific historical setting or a science-fiction piece.**

another version of the same tale, even if the language you use does make it unique to you. It's doubtful that publishers would be interested in an exact retelling of the classic fairy tales. Instead, think of ways to take the essence of the original and turn it into something that even the Brothers Grimm would be surprised at.

SPIN DOCTORS

The easiest place to start is to take the familiar elements of a fairy tale and mutate them in an unexpected and quirky way. What if, for example, Cinderella was the villain of the piece and her stepsisters were actually the good guys? Or if when the prince came to try on the slipper Cinderella realised that she didn't like him much after all? Maybe the seven dwarfs that Snow White meets are actually a platoon of diminutive but deadly assassins who agree to dispatch the wicked queen in a violent military coup and place their new friend on the throne? Read Eugene Trivizas' *The Three Little Wolves and the Big Bad Pig* for a great example of how this works, or watch *Shrek*!

Putting your own spin on a classic story can present it in a whole new light, keeping the enchantment and magic of the original while making it suitable for a new, modern audience. Playing with a reader's expectations in this way allows you to fill a story with humour and surprise, although you should always try and keep the central themes of the tale or children may not identify with it.

MODERN MAGIC

Another way of borrowing from fairy tales is to relocate them in the modern world. If there's one that you particularly love, say *Jack and the Beanstalk*, then you could take the essence of the story and create a novel around it. Jack could be a boy whose family is being threatened by a multinational corporation run by an evil arms dealer known as Gigantous Large. Jack, who has a real knack for understanding technology, finds a way into Large's company headquarters where he risks his life to steal three pieces of valuable technology, using them to expose, and finally destroy, his nemesis. It's easy to transform the bare bones of a classic into a thrilling, futuristic story that publishers will snap up and children will adore.

If you don't want to be restricted to a template in this way, then just use certain elements of a fairy tale and introduce them into the modern world of your story. Eoin Colfer's *Artemis Fowl* books – essential reading for anyone who wants to write a bestseller for children – are populated by 'fairies' who live underground and who possess more advanced technology than humans. Fairy tales belong to us all, so take as much or as little as you want from them and make your own magic.

Discover more about the essence of fairy tales in IDEA 2, *The uses of enchantment.*

Try another idea...

'Literature is an uttering, or outering, of the human imagination. It lets the shadowy forms of thought and feeling – heaven, hell, monsters, angels and all – out into the light, where we can take a look at them and perhaps come to a better understanding of who we are and what we want.'
MARGARET ATWOOD

Defining idea...

How did it go?

Q   **I've lost my collection of fairy tales, can you give me a few prompts?**

A   *OK, try these: the smallest boy in the village goes off to defeat the monster; a clever character tricks the king; a child is born no bigger than a thumb; a wicked fairy puts a curse on a baby because she wasn't invited to the celebration party; a king or queen dresses as a beggar to see how other people will respond; a poor man falls in love with a wealthy woman and goes on a quest to prove himself to her; a woman marries a king who tells her she must never explore a certain part of his castle, but she does and discovers something very strange. These are some of the basic ideas that make up classic fairy tales. Use them as a starter and develop them in a unique way.*

Q   **Should I always start with 'Once upon a time' and end with 'they lived happily ever after'?**

A   *These are the staple bookends, but if you're looking to modernise the story then you're better off without them. After all, the 'once upon a time' may be here and now, and you want people to be in suspense about the ending right up until the last page.*

20

Living a fantasy

Some of the most enduring children's books have been set in fantasy realms – from *The Hobbit* and *The Chronicles of Narnia* to the *His Dark Materials* trilogy.

But creating a realistic world is much harder than just playing Sims.

A great many so-called 'serious' writers turn their noses up at fantasy, but they should know better – the origins of practically all fiction lie in this genre. The earliest stories were attempts to explain the things that baffled humankind, ways to make sense of the mysteries of the world. Why do volcanoes spew fire? Why does the moon change shape? People invented fantastical answers – gods who pulled the sun across the sky and who warred in the heavens, monsters who lived deep beneath the ground always waiting to break free – and in doing so created the roots of all fantasy.

TRUTH VERSUS FACT

There are practically as many different kinds of fantasy world in literature as there are writers who create them. A great many set their stories in these fantastical realms because they think it's easier than researching the real world around them.

Here's an idea for you... **Don't see the process of documenting an imaginary world as a chore – see it as an adventure. Buy a large, leather-bound journal and imagine that you are an explorer visiting the location – a Darwinesque figure who has just discovered a lost world. Let your imagination run wild, draw everything you see in this strange realm and annotate the sketches with notes. Add maps and charts, and immerse yourself in your own creation. You may never use half of this, but the process will help you create a living world.**

If you're one of them, stop right there. Creating an imaginary world isn't just a case of giving everything a weird name and scattering a few dragons about – you have to make it as convincing as the world outside your window. You have to make it real. As Ursula Le Guin claimed, 'For fantasy is true, of course. It isn't factual, but it is true.'

No matter how fantastical the world you are creating, it must have its roots in reality, in truth. It doesn't have to be factual – magic can be real, strange creatures can roam the land, pigs can fly – but it must be familiar enough to readers for them to be able to relate to it. If a world is too strange, if its fundamental nature is so alien that it is barely recognisable, then a reader won't be able to identify with it and will switch off.

THE NEW WORLD

All novelists have to create an entire imagined world, and writing fantasy is no different. You have to create a coherent, consistent world that works according to immutable laws. You have to know every corner of this realm, every detail, because in order for a reader to suspend enough disbelief to be transported to a strange place, it has to be flawless. If you don't have a sensory grasp of your location, you won't be able to describe it convincingly, and there's a danger that fundamental principles will change (from the colour of the skies to the shape of the plants).

Learning to see and describe the ordinary world can help you imagine your fantasy world, so check out IDEA 38, *Tearing down the house*, and IDEA 39, *Open your eyes.*

Try another idea...

LET'S GO EXPLORING

If you're planning to include a fantasy world in your book, then you must start visualising this location long before you begin writing. Start by making a map, fixing towns, deserts, mountains, oceans and so on. This is essential for ensuring that you always know where you are when writing. And don't stop there. Make sketches of the landscape, the plants, the animals and the people and start describing them in your notebook. Use all your senses. What does the air smell like? How hot is the water? How tasty is the local delicacy? What creatures can be heard at night?

Pin these scraps and sketches to the wall until you are surrounded by your world. If you know it intimately then you'll have a vivid picture in your head before you start writing. This way, although the world may not be a factual one, it will be believable – it will ring true. And if you are fascinated by what you find there, then a reader will be too.

'Fantasy's hardly an escape from reality. It's a way of understanding it.'
LLOYD ALEXANDER, children's author

Defining idea...

How did it go?

Q **I've spent days imagining my world and I've got the basics, but I need to give it more depth. Any suggestions?**

A *One good way of adding depth is to think about the myths that exist to explain natural phenomena. Before humans found scientific explanations for things such as the sun and storms, they tried to understand them by telling stories, often involving gods. Pick a natural phenomenon on your world and think of a supernatural explanation for it – a dragon breathing fire inside a volcano, perhaps. These myths can either become part of a character's belief system, or they can be real, but they will help add that depth.*

Q **I've planned out my fantasy world. I've got trees that grow upside down and creatures with a hundred legs. Am I ready to start writing?**

A *Something tells me you might not have put much effort into this. It isn't enough to simply think of weird things, you have to work out why plants and animals in your world have evolved this way. By all means have upside-down trees, but you have to know why they evolved (or were created) this way.*

Q **Are there any easy ways to make people feel at home in your fantasy world?**

A *Yes, try mixing familiar things from real life with elements of fantasy. In Ursula Le Guin's* Earthsea *books real plants and animals mingle with imaginary ones, and in Clive Barker's* Abarat *books there are familiar things like television amongst other dazzling imaginings – allowing readers to ground themselves.*

21

A robot army

Robots, space ships, laser guns – science fiction delights many children. But Buck Rogers is long gone; now you have to think like Stephen Hawking and conduct more research than NASA.

Science fiction may be all about things that are out of this world, but the key to writing it successfully is making sure that your book remains down to earth.

If you want to write science fiction but don't know where to start, then don't panic – good ideas are everywhere. One of the best resources is the plethora of science journals on the market; they contain articles on all the latest scientific research and new gadgets.

GET READING

When I was writing *The Inventors* I spent hours lost inside these magazines realising that every crazy thing I was imagining was also something currently being developed for real. If you see a new discovery that fascinates you – a conscious

Here's an idea for you...

Pick an article in a science magazine that interests you, or a recent news report related to a scientific breakthrough or discovery, and make it the central focus of a science fiction plot. It could be anything, but blow it out of proportion and imagine that it somehow changes the world. Think about how people respond, how they survive, how they feel. When you've got your idea, write some short sketches involving characters from this possible future.

robot, nanotechnology – then think about how it could form the central focus of a science fiction plot. After all, the truth is often stranger than fiction.

If you're writing about the future, science magazines can also help you craft a realistic world. Look at the various directions science is taking us and try and imagine the kind of world that will result. If you ground your futuristic world in real science – cloning, robotics, pollution, space travel – then, whether it's a heavenly utopia or a nightmarish dystopia, it will have the ring of truth.

IT'S A MYTH

Another great source of ideas is mythology. Many of the great science fiction books are actually reworkings of famous legends and folk tales, but disguised in a high-tech future. Characters who set off on long voyages of discovery or magical quests become space explorers seeking a new planet, and the terrible mythological creatures they face are replaced by aliens. The magical items that help a hero on his quest become gadgets like helmets equipped with infrared.

For a great example of how to reinvent mythological stories take a look at Melvin Burgess' *Bloodtide*, which is a vivid, often violent, retelling of the thirteenth-century Icelandic *Volsunga Saga* set in a post-apocalyptic world. Authors like C. S. Lewis also borrowed heavily from ancient myths and religious stories. If there is a classical tale that has always appealed, think of ways it could be transposed to a futuristic setting. If you distil the essence of these timeless fantasies they can work anywhere.

Researching the world of your story can be an adventure in its own right – go to IDEA 10, *Bless you!*, to find out how.

Try another idea...

DEAD WOOKIES

A word of warning – science fiction attracts clichés like flies to a dead Wookie. And the majority are the result of lazy research and imaginations working at half-steam. There's nothing wrong with a story involving people entering a computer game (it's been done excellently in books such as Terry Pratchett's *Only You Can Save Mankind*) or characters travelling through time, but if you don't give it your own unique slant it will appear clichéd.

The secret to creating a believable science fiction story lies with your characters. You have to know them just as well as you know your nearest and dearest, because if they don't act

'*For me science fiction is a way of thinking, a way of logic that bypasses a lot of nonsense. It allows people to look directly at important subjects.*'
GENE RODDENBERRY, creator of *Star Trek*

Defining idea...

realistically in your imaginary world nobody will take them seriously. It's no good having a fearless space captain – he has to be a three-dimensional character with weaknesses and phobias just like everyone else. If not, you end up with Captain Kirk. The more unusual your world, the more 'ordinary' and recognisable your characters have to be.

The other thing to remember is research. Science fiction is so named because it has its roots in something that is possible, that is supported by science – even if it's a science that isn't fully understood yet. Feel free to invent as many crazy gadgets and machines as you like, but base them on something that is real, or plausible. Take a look at Eoin Colfer's *Artemis Fowl* books – the fairy technology he uses is remarkable, but it is all explained in such a way that it could, in theory, exist today.

Q   **I've created a world that developed after a mad scientist made Big Macs come to life. I've spent days researching the chemistry and my story feels like a science journal itself. Any hints?**

How did it go?

A   *A common mistake when writing science fiction is learning exactly how the machines and gadgets and scientific theory in your book work, then stuffing all this information into your writing. The research is, above all, to help you better imagine and describe your world, not so you can show off. Don't tell readers about the process of a rocket's liquid hydrogen and liquid nitrogen igniting, show it in the explosion, in the heat and the sound. And if you do need to describe it, let a character do it through natural speech. Don't get lost in the science; remember that it's still fiction.*

Q   **The technology in my book doesn't actually exist, so can I get away with not thinking too hard about it?**

A   *It's fine if you have a piece of technology in your book which can magically heal all wounds, but most readers, certainly older ones, will want to know at least the fundamentals of how it works. Have a character explain it – it encourages cellular growth generating new tissue to close the wound – or make a joke about it. You don't have to go into detail, but it gives a reader confidence in the book's 'reality'.*

22

Chickens and eggs

One of the greatest challenges when writing any book is trying to decide which comes first – character or plot.

Whichever route you decide to take, always remember that it's your cast that will keep your readers hooked.

It's tempting to assume that because you're writing for children, a plot is more important than the characters who experience it. But even the world's most incredible plot, if populated with cardboard characters, will become duller than a collection of, well, cardboard.

Writing a book that will grip readers throughout isn't just about having an exciting plot. You may have the most thrilling idea – a child who goes to wizard school, or a teenage spy trying to save the world (both of those have already been taken, by the way) – and now you just need to carve out a few generic characters to help the action along.

FLAT-BUSTING

The problem with that approach is that when you create characters purely to serve a function in a story, they risk becoming two-dimensional – and nobody finds it easy to identify with a flat character. Characters designed to fit a certain role can appear

Here's an idea for you...

One of the best ways to get to know characters who aren't fully developed is to try placing them in unusual scenarios. Start off small: write about a number of mundane situations from a character's everyday life – a day in school, perhaps, or a trip to the supermarket. Next, place her in a more dramatic situation, such as a terrorist attack or even an alien invasion. Noting how your character acts will help provide new insight into her personality.

artificial, with no existence or history outside of this particular story. Although the plot may do enough to sustain the reader's attention, a child will struggle to feel anything for the people involved.

Even in the most ridiculously big-budget action film, with explosions every five seconds and a death toll of millions, you are first introduced to the characters and their everyday lives. This creates empathy, which means that you care about what happens to them when the drama starts. The more readers believe in a book's characters, the more they care for them, and the greater their emotional involvement in the plot.

PERSONAL GROWTH

There's nothing wrong with starting with a plot – many of the best children's books begin life this way. But you have to spend as much time getting to know each of your protagonists as you would if you were writing a character-driven novel. This ensures that their actions during the course of the story never seem staged or artificial, and it also ensures that your characters grow through the course of the story. Always remember that even though you may know exactly what your plot might entail, your characters don't, and the events that occur, the obstacles they face, should enable them to evolve like real people. If you don't have a good grasp of who your characters are, then they won't behave or respond in a realistic way when they face these obstacles, they won't develop. No matter how exciting the action, the story won't seem real because your heroes will remain static.

If you're still debating the importance of plots and characters then check out IDEAS 23, *Heroes...* and 24, *And villains!* for ways to develop your cast.

Try another idea...

MINDS OF THEIR OWN

If you have a really strong character but no plot, don't worry. Well-developed characters can become so real in your mind that they create their own stories, and drive them from start to finish. Working out the conflicts and obstacles that characters face during the course of their lives can usually supply numerous plot ideas, and if you know them as though they were real, then the way they confront these problems will seem utterly realistic, and therefore exciting to a reader.

You may even find that your characters have so much depth that they refuse to follow your outline, acting differently to how you expected and taking their own course of action. This is when you know that you've created genuine, three-dimensional people, who won't just do as they are told.

'Plot springs from character... I've always sort of believed that these people inside me – these characters – know who they are and what they're about and what happens, and they need me to help get it down on paper because they don't type.'
ANNE LAMOTT, US author

Defining idea...

How did it go?

Q **If my readers are kids then they'll put up with flat characters so long as the action is exciting enough! Do I really have to bother?**

A *Go and wash your mouth out! Children are extremely perceptive – far more than adults – because they are still learning about social behaviour and the psychology of those around them. If they don't see a recognisable foundation of humanity in a character then they'll switch off. They know what it feels like to be scared, happy, sad, angry, confused. If they don't see similar emotional responses in your characters then the book will be meaningless for them.*

Q **But I'm just writing a picture book! My character only appears on a few pages, and it's a duck. Do *I* have to bother?**

A *You wash your mouth out, too! Even characters in picture books need fully-developed personalities if their reaction to events is to appear genuine. Young readers will be expecting to see elements of themselves on the page, and will be all the more aware if a character is two-dimensional. And even if characters are animals they have to have recognisably human personalities.*

Q **OK, I think my main character is fully developed now. Do I have to take the same care and effort with my secondary cast?**

A *No, you don't have to plan the life story of every evil henchman. Secondary characters can be kept as flat as you like, so long as they are not clichéd stereotypes (er... like evil henchmen). In fact, keeping them relatively flat stops them getting in the way of the action.*

23
Heroes...

Your main characters are the most important element of your book, and getting them right is the difference between ending up in the slush pile or, well, in an ancestral pile.

Your heroes and heroines have to draw readers in, engage their attention from the first page right the way through to the last.

In short, they have to be strong and dynamic, and people that a child can empathise with. Finding this combination can be tricky, but there are some simple techniques to help.

I NEED A HERO

It goes without saying that the principal character in a book has to be the hero or heroine – or both. Usually there is only one main protagonist, and this is a good way to keep a story tight and under control. There's nothing to stop you using two main characters, or even three or four, but you should pick one to be the main focus of the book – the eyes through which the bulk of the plot plays out – otherwise it can become confusing. If you do use more than one protagonist always make sure that they are easily distinguishable – that each looks, speaks and behaves

Here's an idea for you...

In order to make a hero come alive on the page you have to know him as well as you know yourself. Long before you start writing your book you should create a character file, describing his personality, likes and dislikes, dreams and nightmares. Try writing a diary from your character's point of view, describing various important moments. Spend some time each day building and developing his profile in your imagination – when you eventually start your book your hero will instantly spring to life.

in a unique way. This helps keep momentum in the plot and ensures that readers never get muddled about who is who.

In most cases, children like to read about characters that are slightly older than themselves. Heroes in books for eight- to twelve-year-olds, for example, are often in their early teens. There is no hard and fast rule stating that you have to have a young protagonist, however. Jonathan Stroud's excellent *The Amulet of Samarkand* has a genie as one of its two main protagonists, while children will usually empathise with rebels such as Robin Hood or animals that have distinct personalities – anyone that is a child at heart.

PERSONALITY TRAITS

Whoever your heroes are, there are certain steps you have to follow to ensure that a reader will fall in love with them. First, always make them likable and understandable – even if one is a rogue, the core of his personality has to be good. Never make a hero a know-it-all or a goody-two-shoes – this kind of character is repugnant! Heroes should have their faults, because these can become endearing and present them as more rounded personalities. But essentially they should be honest, brave, clever, resourceful, caring, resilient, optimistic and modest, though it may take a while for these qualities to emerge (these character traits were actually discovered as being universally appreciated by kids in a recent survey).

Your main characters should always be somebody, or something, that a reader would like to be, and their adventures should be things that a child would love to do but can't. Wish-fulfilment has played a huge part in the success of characters such as Harry Potter and Alex Rider – what child wouldn't want to be able to cast spells or travel the world as a teenage spy? If a child wants to be in the shoes of a character then you're onto a winner. But you should also always make life difficult for your heroes, as the more the odds are against them, the more a young reader will want to be on their side.

Creating your main character is one thing, but remember that what makes a good hero is a good villain. Take a trip to the dark side in IDEA 24, *And villains!*.

Try another idea...

MR ORDINARY

Another essential key to making your main character popular with your readers is to ensure that he or she starts the story as an average, everyday individual. Children know that they are not perfect, they all have insecurities and worries and times when they feel that they aren't special. If your main characters start off being amazing at everything, or have special powers that make life easy, then a reader may start to despise them rather than empathise with them. If characters start off being ordinary (emphasise this by giving them some very human flaws) then find their own inner strengths and powers by facing up to their problems and challenges, they will be loved.

'If everybody was satisfied with himself there would be no heroes.'
MARK TWAIN

Defining idea...

How did it go?

Q Are there any other ways to get readers to support your character right from the start?

A *Try using sympathy, inequality and danger. These techniques are often employed by screenwriters, who have a really short time to get audiences to like their characters (often only minutes). Try making your main character an undeserved victim of something very early on in the book (think about poor Harry Potter under the stairs). Young readers will sympathise and want to see the character redeemed. Likewise, heroes who are downtrodden, vulnerable or oppressed automatically attract affection and support. Lastly, readers will identify with characters they are worried about, so place a hero in danger right from the start.*

Q Are there any tricks to keeping things simple when using two main protagonists?

A *One of the main problems is knowing how to split the story between them, and which one to follow when they're apart. Making sure you tag along with the right character at the right time can be tricky because if you switch between their storylines at the wrong point it can disturb the momentum of the story, and if one character's adventure is much more exciting it can upset the balance of the book. Give them the same motivation – a shared cause of conflict – and intertwine their stories. Take a look at The Amulet of Samarkand again for a perfect example of how to perfect the balance between characters.*

24

And villains!

The real pulling power of a story lies with the villain. From Voldemort to Darth Vader, giving life to a terrifying and believable baddie is the key to writing a classic.

Good villains are essential because the better your baddies are, the more exciting your main characters become. In short, the better the villain, the better the hero.

But coming up with a good villain is far harder than simply thinking of a force of pure evil and pitting it against your hero. Ambiguous, shadowy villains who never reveal the reason for their wickedness are a cop out for a writer and a disappointment for a reader. Villains need to be as fully developed as protagonists, because it's only when their motives seem real that they truly become terrifying.

JUST ANOTHER EVIL GENIUS

The most important step to creating great villains, who will have readers cowering under their duvets at night, is to make sure they have fully developed characters. Two-dimensional villains like the Bogeyman or an evil genius who just wants to

Here's an idea for you... **It's vital to know everything there is to know about your villain before you start writing. Spend time writing a detailed biography, from childhood right through to the time of the book. Determine what it was that made him or her evil (there is always a reason – nobody is born wicked) and just why your baddie is acting like this. Think about actions (whether blowing up the planet or giving wedgies on the playground) and motives (power, revenge, boredom), and work out what it is about the past that led to them.**

blow up the world for no good reason may seem moderately scary if the book is written well, but if you spend time giving your villains their own fascinating background, worthy goals and believable motivations then they will become much more frightening.

The villain in *The Inventors* is Saint, a crazed billionaire scientist who wants to eradicate life from the planet in order to start again. I put just as much thought into the background of this character as I did my two heroes, until eventually he began to seem real. It was at this point that I realised that the logic Saint uses to rationalise his evil actions actually made sense to me – why not start life again, eliminate war and disease? It was a chilling thought, but it did hammer home the point that the most terrifying villains are those whose motives make sense.

GOOD VERSUS EVIL

A common pitfall with new writers is not matching villain to hero, but there is a good technique for creating the right balance between dark and light. Try giving your villain the same personality as your hero, but twist it. Think of Anakin Skywalker in *Star Wars* – if events in his past had turned out differently then he would have ended up a hero, like Luke. Instead, a growing darkness in his personality caused by events in his youth turned him into Darth Vader, one of the most memorable villains. As an inexplicable force of pure evil, Darth is scary – but as a man twisted by bitterness, whose powers are fuelled by rage, he is terrifying.

One of the best ways to create unforgettable villains is to understand the kinds of things that children are terrified of. Check out IDEA 11, *The Bogeyman cometh.*

Try another idea...

Of course, a villain is usually the complete opposite of a hero – one destroys while the other builds, one harms while the other heals. A baddie should be the nemesis for your protagonists, seeking to block their progress at every stage, providing conflict and intrigue – and should always be wicked. But the reasons for doing this have to be connected to a twisted personality, and personal history, or your villain will seem nothing more than a cookie-cutter criminal. I'm not saying that your villains' actions should be entirely understood – never try and justify them in the hope of being politically correct. They should be evil, but they will always have more power if they are grounded in the truly frightening reality of the human psyche.

Perhaps most importantly, having a villain whose personality and life was once not so different to that of the hero forces your protagonists to question their own motives. In facing such a villain they have to confront the darkness inside themselves – a great way to make a story absolutely riveting.

'You cannot have power for good without having power for evil too. Even mother's milk nourishes murderers as well as heroes.'
GEORGE BERNARD SHAW

Defining idea...

109

How did it go?

Q **I'm a bit nervous about getting inside the head of my villain, and I'm struggling to think about motivation. Are there any good ways to get inside the psyche of a criminal?**

A *The best way, as with every aspect of writing, is to read, read, read. Look at your favourite books and work out what makes the villains so terrifying, so reprehensible and don't be afraid to be inspired. Another method is to watch crime shows on television – anything from* CSI: Crime Scene Investigation *to* The X-Files. *Obviously these programmes are aimed at adults, but they often reveal insights into the minds of criminals and villains which you can use with your own characters. Lastly, try looking at your protagonists. Imagine if life had turned out differently for them, if something had happened to twist their view of the world to such an extent that they turned to violence and crime.*

Q **I quite like the idea of my villain being something that is pure evil, that cannot be explained or understood. Is this OK?**

A *Of course, the idea of pure evil is terrifying, and having a villain or force that can never be understood or explained can create a real sense of intrigue and danger in your book. But often a character like this can seem two-dimensional and wooden – the evil equivalent of a stock action hero. By all means keep your villain's origins and motives a mystery to the reader, but you should know what they are.*

25

I want to be a real boy!

Just because you're writing for a young audience doesn't mean your characters can be wooden. Only when you know them intimately will you be able to cut their strings.

Your characters need to be living and breathing inside your head before you can unleash them on the page.

Literary characters are one of life's great mysteries. Essentially, they exist as nothing more than words, but to a reader they can become more real, more genuine, than an actual human being. This bizarre phenomenon only takes place when an author has an intimate understanding of people – what motivates them, what they think, what their instincts are, how their past has shaped their psyche – building up a realistic portrait of how complex people actually are.

THE HUMAN ZOO

Don't worry, it's not as daunting as it sounds. Creating realistic characters is simply a matter of looking around you. Observe your family and friends, your neighbours, anybody you pass on the street – not just kids, but everybody. Look out for what makes these people tick, their idiosyncrasies, their physical and mental quirks, the

Here's an idea for you...

Write a checklist of every important aspect of a character's life. Start with the basics, such as name, date of birth, physical details, habits, address and so on. Then add more personal information, such as details of parents (their jobs, if they're divorced, does the character get on with them), siblings, the family house, friends and enemies, strengths and weaknesses, skills and interests, favourite films... These can be short, and they don't have to be written in the character's voice, but they'll give you a better idea of a character's life outside of the story.

way they walk, the noise they make when they sneeze – everything! The closer you are to people, the more intimately you can investigate them. What makes them happy, sad, excited, nervous?

Discover the most fascinating aspects of their behaviour and always write these down – using your notes as a catalogue of thoughts, actions and quirks that you can call on to give depth to your characters. If you're struggling to think of characters, then try taking some of your observations and mixing them up, seeing what kind of person emerges. Many of my characters have materialised from a combination of other people's behaviours – a mannerism from one person and a phobia from another, a kind word from him and a twitch from her. If you spend enough time watching people then ultimately characters will form from the patchwork of actions, thoughts, speech and other details that you pick up on, evolving inside your imagination until they develop a life and a personality of their own.

GETTING TO KNOW YOU

Once your characters have started to form, probe their personality and their background, learning all there is to know about them. It may sound a little silly, but interview them. List a series of questions about their life and thoughts and leave spaces for the answers, making sure that you write in their particular voice. Ask about the past, about family, friends, likes and dislikes, thoughts on controversial issues, dreams and nightmares, favourite clothes and games.

People don't always want to reveal their inner motivations, but often their possessions can say more about them than their actions. Check out IDEA 26, *Can I have one?*.

Try another idea...

If you like, turn some of these answers into short sketches from the point of view of a particular character, each describing an important moment. These can be as long or as short as you like, and don't worry too much about the style of your writing – nobody will ever see these exercises except for you. Just try and stay honest to the personality of the characters you are creating and you'll soon know them better than you know yourself.

IT'S ALIVE!

Don't think that just because you know everything there is to know about your characters you have to write it all down in your story. Lengthy character descriptions can be extremely dull, and you should never tell a reader the details of a character's personality. But if you know your creations, then these details will come out effortlessly in the way they act, in the way they speak – they will be shown in a realistic way. If your characters are alive in your head, then they cannot help but come alive on the page.

'It is true that writing is a solitary occupation, but you would be surprised at how much companionship a group of imaginary characters can offer when you get to know them.'
ANNE TYLER, US novelist

Defining idea...

113

How did
it go?

Q   I'm looking for some good ways of getting inside people's heads to find out what they think. Know of any?

A   *One exercise I have great fun with is picking a newspaper story, something juicy and scandalous from the tabloids or from a soap opera. Try to imagine the events detailed from the perspective of one of the people involved, writing a short sketch about what happened and any emotional response to it. Use this as a starting point for getting to know about the character. Use the clues from one you've written to find out more – from reading habits to wildest dreams and biggest regrets. It's a useful method for understanding other people.*

Q   Can I just put my friends and family in my book?

A   *Yes, but it's much harder than creating characters of your own. If you try and fit a person you know intimately into your book then your imagination may be limited by your relationship with that person. A character may not respond in a realistic way to a threat because you can't imagine your friend or family member in that situation. By all means use real people for inspiration, but ensure you don't imitate them completely – your characters should be unique and original.*

26
Can I have one?

Children love to own stuff. Sitting down and working out exactly what your characters want, or already possess, can be the best way to get to know them.

Ask yourself honestly if you can picture the characters that you are planning to write about — or even those that you have already put down on paper.

If the answer is yes, then you shouldn't have any problems answering the following. What do your characters carry in their pockets? What is their favourite item of clothing? What do they clutch at night when they are terrified? What memories flood their imaginations when they look at their favourite toy or photograph? Still think you can picture them? Whatever you are writing, you have to be able to visualise every detail of your characters.

REAL LIFE

You should always remember that your characters are what will bring your book to life. It doesn't matter if you've got the most gobsmacking, flabbergasting plot in the history of literature, if readers don't see a realistic person in a character – someone

Here's an idea for you...

One of the best ways to get to know your characters better, whether it's a new character or one you've been working on for a while, is to write out a list of twenty objects they might wear, own or carry. Don't go into too much depth, just write down whatever comes to mind. Next, write a series of short sketches describing exactly how your character came by these items – taking care to convey what each means and what it would be like if it got lost. These will give you, and your readers, a clearer sense of who your character is.

that they could bump into walking down the street – then they'll drop your book like a poisonous snake.

Children, more than most, look for realism in characters because they observe people with far more care than grown-ups – they are constantly watching, learning, reading their parents and friends because it is part of the way they come to understand the world. As a result every character in your book – whether it's a moody teenager or a fantastic creature like a dragon – must become a real person in the eyes of the reader.

Creating characters with this depth of realism and a believable, three-dimensional existence on the page is one of writing's most difficult challenges. And you can come a cropper by trying *too* hard – setting every detail in stone, inadvertently smothering your creations, making them appear staged and lifeless.

GOTTA PICK A POCKET OR TWO

Creating believable characters is all about finding a balance – and one of the best tricks to help achieve this is to focus on what items your heroes and heroines own. When first starting to visualise your characters, use the phrase 'you are what you own' as a kind of mantra – their belongings can reveal a great deal about who they are, and can be used to subtly convey this information to the reader.

When creating young characters it's vital to know the kinds of objects they carry and clothes they wear. Read IDEA 9, Kidspotting.

Try another idea...

Picture somebody dear to you, somebody you know quite well, and try to visualise this person in your head. What does she carry in her pockets, in her handbag? What can she never leave home without? Painkillers, a lucky key ring, a stone tablet which acts as a gateway to another dimension?

Each piece of clothing people wear, each object they carry, is a choice made by them – a choice which reflects their personality. Tiny snippets like this are essential for creating a character who truly leaps off the page into the reader's imagination. The key is not to list these things – a sure-fire way to make any character seem unrealistic and boring – but to use them to give you a much clearer idea of who you're writing about. By paying close attention to which of these details you reveal, you have control over how readers see and engage with your characters.

Personal items like these can also be used to reveal elements of a character's personality in an inventive way. It's so much more convincing to show a young boy panicking over the thought of losing a penknife given to him by his dead father than it is simply to write about how much he misses his dad. Likewise these objects can be used to raise the tension another notch, especially if we don't know why a character is carrying them.

'Riches do not consist in the possession of treasures, but in the use made of them.'
NAPOLEON

Defining idea...

117

How did it go?

Q **I'm having trouble thinking of the objects, let alone the characters! Everything I've picked seems to be something that I own. Is that OK?**

A *If you think of things that you own then the chances are you'll end up writing about yourself. Try and imagine objects that you find strange and unfamiliar – objects that you wouldn't dream of carrying. There isn't any harm in thinking of things that you own, however, and sometimes this can be a good place to start. But try and picture them from someone else's point of view. Even the most ordinary item in your pocket may have immense emotional significance to somebody else, and it's up to you to work out why.*

Q **Can I think of objects first, then build somebody around them?**

A *You're the boss! You can have great fun trying to create a person around a group of random objects, especially if you're having trouble imagining a character. Ask a friend to write down a list of twenty random objects, making them as wild or as dull as they like. Then create a character who would use all these items, inventing a history and describing this individual's appearance and personality. Although you might not end up with somebody you can actually use in a story, it's all good practice, and it can be great fun!*

27

Treat 'em mean

It sounds like an exercise in pure cruelty – creating characters you feel emotionally attached to and then throwing problems at them. But all good children's books are driven by conflict.

Conflicts and complications form the heart of every good story — characters encounter a problem or obstacle and ultimately resolve it through their own actions.

By making things hard for your heroes you're giving them the opportunity to grow and develop. By forcing them to face up to conflict – whether it's a global threat or a personal dilemma – you allow them to become stronger, better people. In creating a near-impossible journey you let your characters make choices, and it is through this conflict and resolution process that they show their true colours. If they aren't driven by these conflicts then they just won't be real.

A ROCKY START

Although there should be a number of conflicts in the book, the first one your main character will encounter is that of the critical situation – the important event or decision at the beginning of the story where your character's life changes. If you're

Here's an
idea for
you...

Before you start writing, get to know what your main character's goals are and make a list. Look into his history and find the cause of his ambitions and insecurities, adding a brief explanation to your list. When you know exactly what a character is striving for, work out what path he would have to take to get to accomplish any goal – and for each goal add several things that would stand in the way. Use this list to help plot your story.

writing a plot-driven novel, then you'll already know what this is – a death in the family, moving to a new school, being abducted by aliens. This crisis is what propels the book into motion and is usually beyond your hero's control – he's thrust into this situation, and the way he deals with it is what pulls the plot along from page to page.

This initial conflict provides the framework of the story – it's what makes the period between the first page and the last page of the book different to any other time in the character's life. But since this main obstacle won't be overcome until the end of the book, you have to create other challenges. By generating new, increasingly more difficult problems in every chapter, raising the stakes for a character throughout the story, you will fill your reader with suspense and apprehension. The harder you make things for a main character, the more readers will become involved in the story. So as soon as a character has overcome one problem, provide an even greater challenge.

PERSONALISED PROBLEMS

If you're not sure about how to handle conflict, then remember that obstacles are always related to goals. In plot-driven stories, these goals will stem from the critical situation, and often involve characters trying to get life back to normal or defeat some terrible threat – or both. If you're not yet sure of your plot, then it's still important to work out what your characters' goals are, because only then will you know what to throw in their way.

Learn what kinds of problems kids face in IDEA 17, *Problem child*.

Try another idea...

All children have goals, and it's often the pursuit of these that creates inner conflict and causes feelings of doubt and insecurity. It's essential that you work out what your characters want, what they strive for, what they would change if they could, because only then will you know what obstacles to hurl at them, what internal and external struggles will really challenge them.

FREEDOM FIGHTERS

The most important thing to remember about conflict is that it's the way your characters deal with it which makes a story interesting. Only by knowing them as well as you know yourself will you ensure that they overcome each challenge realistically and change as individuals. If you know your characters well enough then they will respond to a problem in their own way – using methods that might just surprise you. The more you know about them, the greater the sense of freedom and motivation they will have, meaning that their solutions to problems will never seem staged and artificial.

Poorly thought-out characters will always meet and overcome conflict in a predictable way. Characters with depth and past lives, however, will seem genuine even when all the odds are against them.

'Often I'll find clues to where the story might go by figuring out where the characters would rather not go.'
DOUG LAWSON, US writer

Defining idea...

How did it go?

Q   **Is there a good way to think up terrible tortures for my characters?**

A   *Try asking yourself these questions. What could go wrong when your characters pursue their goals? Who or what stands in their way? When could be the worst possible time for something to happen? Where does something go wrong? And how could things go wrong (what twists of fate could create setbacks)? Thinking about each conflict this way can help you get a better idea of each obstacle.*

Q   **Great, I've sorted out all of the external conflicts, but I'm not sure about the internal ones. Can I just not bother with those?**

A   *Internal conflicts are problems and insecurities that your characters have, and which are brought to light when the external conflict kicks off. By dealing with external struggles, characters come to confront their own inner conflicts, and by triumphing over them they are able to grow. Without inner conflict, your characters have no depth, and their actions will appear false to a reader. Without external conflict there is no plot, only a character's angst. You have to have both in order to make a story work.*

Q   **Do characters always have to *overcome* problems?**

A   *No. Don't be afraid to let them fail to surmount some. In doing so they may learn something important about themselves, or set up a challenge that proves even more dramatic.*

28

Speak up!

Kids can spot impostors from a mile off, especially if they talk funny. Here's how to prevent your beautifully rounded characters falling apart every time they open their mouths.

Look at any novel for children and you'll see just how much information is conveyed through dialogue.

But dialogue is easy, right? I mean, surely it's just a case of listening to how people speak to each other then transcribing it onto the page. Unfortunately, it isn't as simple as this because the secret of effective dialogue in fiction is not to emulate real speech, but to give the *impression* of real speech.

VERBAL DIARRHOEA

If that sounded a little confusing, try remembering the last conversation you had. When you were talking, it probably seemed quite a short piece of dialogue, but if you were to transcribe it onto a page it would seem ridiculously longwinded. In real conversations, people hesitate, stammer, repeat themselves, stop halfway through a

Here's an idea for you...

Record two or more people in conversation (it's best to use real people, but if you use a television programme make sure it's an unscripted chat show or documentary), then write down the conversation word for word. Rewrite the dialogue as though you were using it in a book, adding action and attributive verbs. Notice how much you have to cut out before the speech looks realistic on the page. If in doubt, try reading it out loud.

sentence, digress, contradict themselves, talk over one another and waffle on until the cows come home. And if you try to imitate this then your book will be a thousand pages long and totally unreadable.

If you mimic real speech when writing then it will look artificial, because the rules that govern speech on the page are very different to those that control real-life conversations. As a writer, you have to pare down every single piece of dialogue so that it is short and to the point, as this keeps up the pace and prevents the reader getting bogged down in paragraphs of unnecessary speech. Dialogue serves two main functions in fiction – it drives the plot along and it deepens a reader's understanding of the characters. Ask yourself, of every piece of dialogue you use, which of these functions it performs. If the answer is neither, then chances are it is just extraneous waffle, and should be cut.

Oh, and while we're on the subject of dialogue, never use it for gratuitous exposition. If you provide too much information through a character's speech then it will be obvious to a reader that you're using the character as a tool. Any realism will be lost and a reader will be jolted out of your story faster than a four-year-old on a rodeo bull.

SAY WHAT?

Another vital thing to remember when writing
dialogue is that characters must express
themselves in a unique way. In real life,
everybody's patterns of speech are subtly different, and if this isn't reflected in your
cast then a reader will struggle to remember who's who, especially in scenes with
lots of talking. When creating your characters, think carefully about the way they
speak. Are they shy or outgoing? Serious or clownish? It's always useful to practise
writing dialogue for specific characters long before you start your book, so that their
speech sounds as natural as possible on the page.

Above all, always try and keep a sense of momentum in your dialogue. Keeping
speech short – the golden rule is no more than three uninterrupted sentences per
character – provides a sense of pace, while regularly altering which character is
speaking provides the illusion of movement. If you've given one of your characters
large chunks of speech then consider breaking
it up by sharing it with another character –
even if the other character is just interrupting
with questions. 'Alternatively, use actions to
break up the dialogue and ground speech in
the real world,' he said, saving his work and
gulping down the last of his tea.

**Try having a few conversations
with your characters while
reading IDEA 25, *I want to be a
real boy!***

Try
another
idea...

**'It usually takes more than
three weeks to prepare a
good impromptu speech.'**
MARK TWAIN

Defining
idea...

125

How did it go?

Q   This might be a bit basic, but should I be using 'said' all the time?

A   *There's nothing wrong with the word 'said'. It's the writer's staple, and because it is so familiar to a reader it becomes almost invisible if used correctly. Your job is to transport the reader into the story, and using 'said' can help make the dialogue flow. There's no need to use it after every piece of speech, however – if there are only two characters talking then just add it now and again as a reference point. If there are more characters then use 'said' more often, or better still add actions instead. '"No way!" She picked up the knife. "I won't let you."'*

Q   Can't I just use other attributive verbs?

A   *If you're trying to think of as many ways as possible to attribute speech, then stop! It's the mark of an amateur to substitute 'said' with 'whooped', 'cheered', 'observed', and so on. Use a different verb now and again, but using them all the time will draw a reader's attention away from the story. It's always best to convey the mood of the speech in the speech itself.*

Q   What about adverbs?

A   *There's no need to write something like '"I miss him so much," she said sadly.' Many new writers refuse to leave adverbs alone, and their dialogue becomes tedious – even to young readers. If emotion is present in the speech, it doesn't need to be reiterated.*

29

Staying alive

It's all very well knowing your hero intimately, but this is only the beginning.

No matter how well you visualise your characters, if you can't bring them to life on the page then it's about as exciting as a dusty waxwork in Madame Tussauds' basement.

A great many new writers (myself included at one point) assume that making a character seem realistic and exciting is all about description – in much the same way as many Victorian novels, which often devote thousands of words to describing a character in immaculate detail, right down to the stitching on a girdle. Adults will often appreciate the worthy struggle of poring through information like this. Children won't. So try these other techniques for the kiss of life.

STATIC SHOCK

Description is largely passive, and too much of it at any point of the book can risk boring a reader to tears. 'The boy walked into the clearing, wearing a faded red T-shirt and ripped jeans, holding a baseball cap in his hand.' Heavy description like

Here's an
idea for
you... **Try experimenting with these methods of bringing a character to life: description, interjection, action, association, thoughts, speech and reaction. Take a character and write several sketches each using a different balance of these methods – more description in one piece, more action in another – until you find the combination that works best for you. Try to imagine what the reader wants to be told or shown, and what can be left to the imagination.**

this conveys a great deal of information, but it is static and unnecessary. Pick up on the most essential elements of description and any imaginative young reader will fill in the blanks: 'The boy staggered into the clearing, his baseball cap clutched against the blood stains on his T-shirt.'

AND ACTION!

Careful description like this is the foundation of a character's presence on the page, but other techniques evolve these foundations into something that appears to live and breathe. 'His whole body was in agony, the wound in his chest unbearable. He could barely see, but he knew they were watching him – the coven of worshippers who were anxiously retreating from the sacrificial altar.' Interjections like this are another form of description but they reveal the character's state of mind, his thoughts, adding depth and mystery to the scene.

Physical action is the best way to bring a character to life – it creates a more dynamic picture than passive description and is far more convincing than any interjection by the author. 'He moved towards them, his feet slipping on the crimson mud beneath his bare feet. Some of the worshippers screamed as he pulled the golden knife from his pocket, pointing it unsteadily at the head priest.'

GUILTY BY ASSOCIATION

A more subtle form of description is association, which leaves the interpretation to readers, rather than simply providing them with a list of physical attributes. 'The worshippers could all see the runes that decorated the length of the blade, reflecting an unearthly light, and the photograph of his dead brother which was wrapped around the handle.' These may only be small details, but they have vital associations to the character's motives and psychology. Do the runes signify the boy's power? Does the photo justify his revenge?

If you only remember one thing when writing, it's show, don't tell. Find out more in IDEA 45, _Showing off_.

Try another idea...

TALKING HEADS

Allowing a reader access to your character's thoughts also brings him to life on the page. Use interior monologues to convey information that cannot be ascertained by description or action. _'Just a few more minutes_, he thought as he stepped forward, trying to control the power that surged from the knife, flooding his body. _I'm finally going to kill him.'_ And, of course, actual speech can be used to reveal more about a character. '"It's time," he shouted as the head priest collapsed to his knees. "You never should have killed my brother."'

'**Don't say it was "delightful"; make us say "delightful" when we've read the description. You see, all those words (horrifying, wonderful, hideous, exquisite) are only like saying to your readers "Please will you do the job for me."'**
C. S. LEWIS

Defining idea...

Lastly, use reaction to further develop your character's presence – revealing more about looks and personality through the eyes and thoughts of others. 'The priest didn't know how the boy was still alive. Blood was flowing from his wound and his skin was deathly white, but his eyes burned fiercely – possessed by the power of the knife. "Luke," he hissed, raising his arms in defence. "We didn't kill him, you did!"' Just always be careful not to switch viewpoints too much or it might get confusing.

Q   **I think I'm getting the hang of balancing the different ways of bringing characters to life, but I've written the same scene so many times I'm sick of it! Can I try something else?**

A   *Sure! If things are getting a little samey then try putting your characters in a completely different scene – either something else from your novel or something random from another genre entirely. Try placing your hero in a packed elevator which has just broken down, or at a family reunion where he has to give some bad news. Each scene will have a different mood and pace, letting you see which methods of bringing your character to life work best. If the way you describe your character varies, try to work out why.*

Q   **I've had a go at using association but it's turned out cheesy. Is there a golden rule?**

A   *Try reversing typical associations. We associate certain actions and objects with various types of people, but if every character with a crucifix around their neck was a devout Catholic then our characters would be clichéd and stereotypical. Always try and surprise the reader.*

Q   **Can't I just scrap all this and tell readers what happens using description?**

A   *That would be a newspaper report, not fiction. Children don't want to be told what's going on, they want to see it, to imagine they're there.*

How did it go?

30

Who's in charge?

Every piece of writing has to have a viewpoint, and choosing between a first-, third- or even second-person narrator can be the most important decision you'll ever make.

The point of view you select to tell your story is essential because it's the window that looks out onto your literary world.

And if this window isn't in the right place to best appreciate the view then there's no point in writing at all.

I SPY

Let's start off with the most personal perspective: the first person. If you write from this point of view then the entire story is narrated by a single character. Everything in the book is seen through a single 'I', each event in the story is filtered through the mind and voice of this narrator, and is shaped by a limited understanding.

The biggest strength of a first-person narrative is that it is an extremely immediate and accessible form in which to write. Readers quickly identify with the narrator because the story is told from such an intimate perspective – the key character

Here's an idea for you... **If you're finding it difficult to separate yourself from a first-person narrator, try writing sketches where you meet your creation. Start by writing about the meeting from your own point of view, then from the point of view of your character – using first person both times. This should help you pick out the important differences between you and your protagonist.**

becomes a friend, an accomplice. Darren Shan's excellent 'autobiographical' vampire books are a perfect example – readers very quickly come to see the tormented main character as a close acquaintance, and when the action starts it is impossible not to feel drawn in.

It doesn't take much to see how well the first person can work. Which sounds more immediate, more intense: 'she leapt for the ledge just as the bomb detonated behind her' or 'I leapt for the ledge, just as the bomb detonated behind me'? When you write in the first person, your narrator is immersed in the action, and so is the reader.

BLINKERED

There are problems with this point of view, however. Readers can only know as much about the story as the character knows, they can only experience what the character experiences. There are ways around this, however, especially if the narrator is relating a story that has already happened. You can use phrases such as 'I later found out that...' and 'If I knew then what I knew now...' to convey vital information, but don't overdo it.

On top of this, a reader also has no idea how reliable the narrator is. Think about the last anecdote you told, and how much you embellished it to sound cool in front of your peers. It's vital to work out before you start writing just how much your character knows, and how close to the truth this is.

TRADING PLACES

Another thing you must bear in mind if you take the first-person approach is that the narration has to sound like it is coming from the main character, and not you. If that is a thirteen-year-old girl then you have to enter her head, read her mind, know which words and sentence structures she uses, what mental processes she goes through and how somebody of this age would genuinely react to events. The same goes for any character – a six-year-old narrator will have a completely different view of events to that of a sixteen-year-old, and you have to know where these differences lie.

The biggest pitfall when writing in the first person comes when you cannot separate the story's narrator and your own personality. Because the 'I' is so familiar you can easily find that your individual, unique character has disappeared, and instead it is *you* telling the story – with your voice and your opinions. Your young readers will know that the character is a charade and they'll hate it. The only way to ensure this doesn't happen is to know your main character even better than you know your closest friend. A strong, well-rounded character won't ever lose that uniqueness.

Before you start writing in the first person you have to climb inside the head of your protagonist. Try IDEA 25, *I want to be a real boy!*.

Try another idea...

'Give a man a mask and he will reveal himself.'
OSCAR WILDE

Defining idea...

How did
it go?

Q **The character I'm using is totally different to me. How can I make her seem realistic?**

A *If you're struggling, then are you sure you want to try and write a whole novel from the perspective of this character? Don't give up just because you think she's completely different; in fact, you stand a much better chance of creating a realistic character because there won't be the same temptation to put yourself in there. Just make sure you know your character inside out before you start writing – try writing a diary from her point of view.*

Q **I enjoy writing in the first person but there's one thing I'm never sure about: how can my character describe herself without resorting to the cliché of looking in a mirror?**

A *Avoid the old 'reflection' technique like the plague. Instead, try letting your character find a photograph of herself when she was a toddler – have her think or talk to somebody about how she looks now in comparison. Or let her meet someone and worry about her appearance, slipping in some subtle description. Many first-person narrators address the reader as a friend, so you could also just have her talk freely about the way she looks, so long as it's in context.*

Q **Should I ever brave the second-person viewpoint?**

A *Anyone who read* Fighting Fantasy *books as a kid is familiar with the second-person viewpoint, which makes the reader the centre of the action. Play around with this style with shorter pieces of writing, but it's probably wise to stay clear of it in a novel.*

31

Third time lucky

Writing in the third person is considered the easiest way to tell a story, but you have to decide if you're going to limit yourself, or go all out and play God.

Take a look at the majority of children's books and you'll see that they're written from a third-person perspective, with the narrator a middleman between the action and the reader.

This format has been used to tell stories for millennia, and because we are so used to hearing the third person it has almost become invisible. This is one of its main benefits – by writing in the third person you're allowing people to forget about the structure of the story and focus on the action.

PLAYING GOD

In this holiest of all viewpoints – the third-person omniscient – your narrator sees everything. This approach gives you limitless freedom to explore everyone and everything in your story, delving into the heads of different characters, switching scenes as often as you like, and taking a break from the story altogether to look at something completely unrelated to your plot and its cast.

Here's an idea for you...

Writing successfully in the third-person limited is about keeping the essence of a first-person narrative but staying one step back. Find an exciting, emotionally charged extract from a novel written in the first person, and rewrite it in the third-person limited, trying to keep the same sense of originality and idiosyncrasy. You can also try writing the same scene from the third-person omniscient, where you can see everything. Which of your rewrites packs more of a punch?

When you've crafted a whole imaginary world and filled it with your own characters it can be tempting to be left to explore it as freely as you like. But this freedom is also the third person's biggest problem, and can easily lead to a lack of engagement with the world you're describing. If you're not focusing on one or two protagonists then a reader won't have an emotional handle on the story and won't feel involved. You can be so engrossed with your Godlike duty of seeing everything and infiltrating every mind that you've missed what's important.

ONE TO ONE

Just because you write in the third person, however, doesn't mean you have to impersonate the Almighty. If you want to tell your story from a personal viewpoint but need to switch between two or more main characters, or peek over the shoulder of your hero every now and again to see what lies ahead, then you can have your cake and eat it – by using the third-person limited.

With this approach, the narrator is still a separate entity from the protagonist (you use 'he' and 'she', not 'I'), but omniscience is limited – the world is only seen from one particular viewpoint, from close behind a single character. The narrator can only enter the head and read the thoughts of that one individual, and is so entwined in the character's thoughts that they are practically inseparable. This helps preserve a greater sense of mystery and drama because a narrator only knows what the character knows, and is in just as much danger of being blindsided.

If you're using the third person but there are too many characters clamouring for attention, then read IDEA 32, Avoiding the squeeze.

Try another idea...

STICK TOGETHER

If you do go with the third-person limited then it's vitally important that you decide right from the start just how limited your narrator is going to be. If he can only see from the viewpoint of a single character then this must *always* be the case – you can't restrain a narrator to the head of a single character for much of a novel then suddenly have him report a future event or delve into the mind of somebody else. This will always jerk a reader out of the story, and could make them feel cheated by the narrator's sudden Godlike powers.

JOIN THE CLUB

Of course, you can use the third-person limited but tell the story from the minds of several different characters. This is extremely useful when the story involves a great deal of simultaneous activity, and when the narrative needs to switch back and forth between your protagonists. Alternating narrators is an excellent way to build up dramatic tension and suspense. Remember that you can only ever use one narrator at a time – always use a new chapter, or at least a break, before switching to another.

'Luke, you'll find that many of the truths we cling to depend greatly upon our own point of view.'
Obi-Wan Kenobi, in *Return of the Jedi*

Defining idea...

How did
it go?

Q I've tried all of the narrative styles but can't decide which one I prefer. How can I be sure?

A Deciding on which viewpoint to pick is a difficult decision, one which will profoundly affect your work, but the effort will ultimately pay off. The best thing to do is to try writing the same scene several times using different viewpoints, and decide which one works best. Listen to your inner voice. The chances are that you already have a strong intuition about which narrative style to use. Keep writing, and if it starts to feel wrong then try something else.

Q And what if I've written the whole book from the wrong viewpoint?

A If you finish your book and realise that it would pack more of a punch if narrated from a different viewpoint then there's only one option. It may take forever, but changing it will produce a better book (and, no, you can't just change all the 'I's to 'he's and 'she's or vice versa). And keep the original!

Q When using the third person, am I allowed to take a sneaky peak into the mind of my villain?

A Of course, although be careful. If you're writing a mystery then a glance into everybody's heads will quickly reveal who the baddie is (if you look into every character except one it will spoil things, too). If you're writing in the third-person limited, however, there's nothing to stop you following the villain some of the time. Look at Clive Barker's Abarat series for a good example.

32

Avoiding the squeeze

When characters are fighting for attention, a piece of fiction can start to resemble a bouncy castle with too many children – sweaty, noisy and horrible to be in.

One unmistakable sign of a new writer is when there are too many voices in your text. To stop this you have to seriously clamp down on freedom of speech.

To ensure that your book is clear and fast paced at all times, it's essential that you only let your main protagonist (or two, if you've gone for this approach) hold the reins. Secondary characters may demand the right to take control of the narrative at times, but if you give in to them then there's a danger that everybody will start talking and all you'll have is chaos. Make sure you're clear right from the start whose story you're telling, and either hand out gags to everybody else, or make them 'disappear' in true dictator style.

TOO MANY COOKS

Once you get the hang of creating characters, it can become a bit addictive. It's tempting to keep increasing the number of main and support characters, fleshing out every single person with the aim of building a more rounded world. From here

Here's an idea for you...

Think of a scene which involves a number of different characters. Start by making brief outlines of every character involved, then work out the best viewpoint to tell the story from. Try writing the scene switching back and forth between the heads of several of the characters, then write it again from the viewpoint of a single one, trying to convey the emotions of the rest of the group from this individual's point of view.

it's only a short hop to leaping in and out of these characters' heads until readers have completely forgotten whose story you're telling.

Always remember, you only ever need the number of characters necessary to make your story work, no more. And your story should only be told through the senses and thoughts of your main protagonist(s). I've read so many manuscripts where the narrative suddenly switches to the viewpoint of a minor character – someone who was just watching an action scene, for example, or even a shopkeeper who has sold a hero something.

This can be okay for subtle references – 'The shopkeeper watched the girl walk out of the store then reached for the phone. *She's way too young to be buying that much fertiliser*, he thought as he dialled the police.' But it can be extremely confusing if almost all of the action is seen through the eyes of one character, but jumps to another every now and again. The same sense of danger and mystery can be kept by staying inside the head of the main character: 'She walked nervously out of the door, casting one look behind her to see the shopkeeper reach for the phone. She shouldn't have ordered so much. She was going to be caught.'

ONE AT A TIME!

You can face a similar problem when you have more than one main protagonist in your book. If your two heroes spend all their time together then who exactly is telling the story? There is always a temptation to switch back and forth between the heads of two different characters faster than a pinball stuck between two pegs, which can be extremely confusing:

'Candy couldn't wait any longer. Taking a deep breath she leant over and gave Adam a kiss on the lips. Adam squirmed away. He wanted Candy to kiss him, but not right now, not in front of his mum and grandma. He wiped his cheek, taking a sip from his drink to conceal his embarrassment. Candy sat back. She couldn't believe she'd been rejected. Adam's grandma watched the two young lovers and smiled, remembering when she was their age.'

Getting your characters to work smoothly together on the page means learning how to show things rather than tell them. Get some tips in IDEA 45, *Showing off*.

Try another idea...

A SMOOTH RIDE

If you force readers to jump in and out of various characters then they will soon grow tired and irritable. Develop a single, strong narrative voice by picking one character to tell the story. In *The Inventors* the two heroes Nate and Cat are inseparable, they do everything together, but the story is told from Nate's point of view – only his thoughts and feelings are openly described in the narrative, while hers are inferred from speech and action. Simply put, a single viewpoint provides a smoother ride.

'Things fall apart; the centre cannot hold; Mere anarchy is loosed upon the world.'
WILLIAM BUTLER YEATS

Defining idea...

How did it go?

Q Can I have two strong narrative voices?

A *Sure! The idea of having one is to keep things simple in your head and give you better control over the pace. There's nothing wrong with having two or more protagonists but each one should have a strong voice, and you should be careful when you switch between them. Make sure you separate your narrative voices with chapters, or at least paragraph breaks, so that your characters share the adventure rather than fight for attention.*

Q I've got a number of main characters but it's getting out of hand. Any advice?

A *One of the biggest pitfalls of creating characters is taking on too many and trying to give them all space in your book. Pick some of the weaker characters and reduce their story to a subplot – one that is seen through the eyes of the characters you allow to remain central.*

Q I want to show how every character is feeling but I also want to stay in the third-person limited. Is there any way to do this?

A *You don't have to get inside a person's head to know how they're feeling – show the fury in the gaze, for instance. You could also use the odd adverb – obviously, clearly, probably – but don't overdo it. It's better to show than to tell.*

33

The Magnificent Seven

Fiction without a plot resembles a car without wheels – if you ignore it then your characters aren't going to budge an inch.

It's all very well having an idea, but in order for that idea to become a book then it has to grow into a story, and from there into a plot.

If you're not sure how to go about this, however, don't worry – much of the hard work has already been done.

Being struck by inspiration is great! You suddenly have a wonderful idea cartwheeling around inside your imagination that is perfect for a book. But knowing where to go with it next can be tricky. When I first thought of *The Inventors* it was a flash of inspiration – two kids who were brilliant inventors and whose love of creating whacky machines and gadgets could land them in all sorts of trouble. This initial premise was great, but it wasn't a story.

Here's an idea for you... **If you've got the spark of an idea for a book, but are not sure how to develop it, then look at the seven classic plots and ask yourself if any could serve as the cornerstone. Try turning your idea into a story using the 'Quest' plot, for instance – use all seven if you like. Each should give you a completely different story. Pick the one you like most, or mix and match from two or more, and work with it. It may completely change, but it's a great place to launch a story from.**

WE DEAL IN LEAD, MY FRIEND

When you're in the process of turning an idea into a story, it's always useful to look at the Magnificent Seven. Nope, I don't mean watching Yul Brynner and his posse fighting bandits, I'm talking about the seven basic plots that can be found in a huge number of novels. Of course, these aren't the only plots in existence, but they're a great place to start when searching for ways to develop your initial concept.

In a nutshell, these plotlines are as follows. The first is 'Defeating the Monster'. It's a tale of conflict, where the hero faces a terrible threat, fights for his life, narrowly escapes death and ultimately saves his family, home or the world from evil. The second is the 'Rags to Riches' story, where downtrodden, unfortunate characters eventually reveal inner strength and beauty to win the day.

Number three is the 'Quest', which sees the hero and his allies travelling the world in order to defeat evil or acquire some sort of treasure – from finding a magical stone that will stop a crazed warlord to tracking down a missing parent. Closely related to this is the 'Voyage and Return', where the protagonist leaves behind his normal life – either voluntarily or against his will – and enters an alien world, only returning when he makes a death-defying escape.

In addition there is 'Comedy', which usually involves confusion getting in the way of a character's goals, but which ends happily; 'Tragedy', which is often related to a character trying too hard for an unattainable goal and failing; and 'Born Again', where a character realises he has to change profoundly in order to get what he wants and live happily ever after.

Before you try and plan your story, you have to think of an idea! Read IDEA 5, *Finding Harry...*, for some tips.

Try another idea...

JUMP START

Depending on who you ask, there are countless other plots available, but many have their roots in the Magnificent Seven. You're not simply looking to pick a plot and mould your idea into it, but use these classic, time-tested stories as a starting place. They should help you get a rough idea of the plot you want to use for your book, letting you get started with some knowledge of where you're going. As soon as you start writing, your own creativity will take over, your characters will grow in their own way and your plot will evolve into something unique.

'To produce a mighty work, you must choose a mighty theme.'
HERMAN MELVILLE

Defining idea...

HIDDEN AGENDA

When you're deciding which direction to take your idea in, it's also useful to think about the theme of your work. This is the abstract idea that forms the heart of your book – friendship, the battle between good and evil, finding inner strength, a quest for identity and so on. The theme of your book is never explicitly stated, but you should know what message you're trying to convey, and each scene in the book should help reinforce it.

How did
it go?

Q   Are there any more classic plotlines I can work with?

A   *These are all related to the seven classic plots but the slight variations
     might inspire you. Faust, with a character who has made a terrible deal he
     can't escape from; Rebellion, with a character who seeks to undermine
     authority; Mystery stories, where the reader follows the clues to try and
     work out whodunit; Rise and Fall (and Rise), where a character loses
     everything and must gain it again; Rite of Passage, which shows the
     difficulties of growing up; the Switch, where two characters trade places...*

**Q   I'm getting a bit lost in all these plots and I'm worried that my
     idea isn't going to be original or unique. Can you throw me a line?**

A   *Sure, just remember that whatever plot you decide to use, it's your
     characters and their choices which will make it work. Ultimately they'll
     create their own paths and lead the action, and this means your idea will
     always be original and unique. Just write from the heart.*

**Q   The theme of my book is going to be friendship. Should I tell
     people this in the first paragraph?**

A   *Never tell readers what your theme is because doing so will spoil their fun.
     Theme is always related to the development and transformation of your
     main characters, and it should only be shown in their actions and choices.
     Never state that 'friendship can often be found in the unlikeliest of places',
     show it by having a character make an unusual friend.*

34

Are we there yet?

Trying to keep track of events in a novel is like trying to run from Land's End to John O'Groats without a map and wearing a blindfold.

But getting lost or bored isn't inevitable — there are ways to always know where you are going.

It's totally understandable that as soon as you've got an idea, or have thought of some interesting characters, you just want to start, well, *writing*. But don't begin until you've at least thought of an outline.

I'm not saying you have to dictate the events of your entire story with precision. If you set everything in stone before you start writing then it's pretty much guaranteed that your book will seem stilted and your characters artificial. But if you have no idea about where you're going then there's just as much chance that your book will either bore readers to tears or lose them completely.

DEM BONES

At its most basic, a plan is simply the bare bones of your story. It should include the initiating event – the 'big bang' that opens the story, which kick-starts everything

Here's an idea for you...

Don't just write an outline on a sheet of paper – this makes it static and difficult to change. Use separate index cards or blank sheets of paper for each scene (it's much easier to think of your book as a sequence of scenes than chapters). Pin the first scene and the last scene at opposite ends of a bare wall then add the others in between, and include material like maps and photos. This gives you an excellent overview and allows you to change scenes around, remove them or add new ones.

else into action and disrupts the life of your main character. It gets the ball rolling, forcing your characters out of their everyday world into the thick of whatever it is you've got in store for them.

Your plan should also include your characters' quest. This doesn't mean they have to look for the Holy Grail, but the initiating event will have triggered a want or need in them – goals that they will only reach towards the end of the book. If you know what a character is seeking then you will always stay true to this, rather than sliding off at a tangent. Being aware of these aims also allows you to plan in obstacles and challenges, resistance that your character has to overcome. These setbacks – and the choices and actions they provoke – are what drive a story forwards, and if you plan at least the major ones before you start writing then you'll have an excellent idea of the shape and pacing of your book.

An outline should also include the ending, even if this is just a vague notion that may change. If you know a main character's goals, and the hurdles that prevent her from reaching them, then the chances are you'll have a rough idea of the final challenge, the one that will make up the climax (where she goes head to head against the evil genius or makes one last attempt to impress her dream guy). Having this climax in your outline means that the rest of your story leads inexorably towards it, building tension and driving it forwards.

WRITING BY NUMBERS

Don't try and flesh out these bare bones too much when creating your outline – if you do then your story will be the literary equivalent of painting by numbers, and will look just as rubbish when it's finished. If every last detail of your plot is set in stone then your characters won't have a chance to surprise you – or the reader. You might find that the way you thought your heroine would deal with a challenge is actually completely wrong, that it would be totally out of character for her to act the way she does in your outline.

When this happens, never try and force your characters to follow your plan – it will be clear even to the youngest readers that your heroes or villains are simply doing what is expected of them. Always let your characters lead you, even if it is into unexpected places – their actions may reveal a much better direction. If they do, change your synopsis, think about how this new turn of events affects the ending and the nature of any quest.

Having an outline is a safety net, something to turn to if you feel that your writing is losing focus or momentum or turning into waffle because you don't quite know where you're going. It's common to be wary of too much planning, but remember that you control the outline, it doesn't control your story.

All stories need to have a beginning, a middle and an end – so start with IDEA 35, *The Big Bang*.

Try another idea...

'For all my longer works, for example novels, I write chapter outlines so I can have the pleasure of departing from them.'
GARTH NIX

Defining idea...

How did
it go?

Q **I've assembled my plot cards and related paraphernalia. But it's looking a little bare. Should I be fleshing it out somehow?**

A *If each index card says something along the lines of 'character x rushes to character y's rescue' then you're probably focusing too much on plot and not enough on your characters. Remember, your main characters have to be given freedom to act as their personalities dictate; they must grow, develop and respond to problems naturally. So when plotting don't just focus on an external action, but consider your characters' emotions, feelings, thoughts and fears. Make notes on each index card about how your characters might feel at this stage of the story. Considering these touches when creating your outline will ensure that the story will develop much more naturally.*

Q **I've just taken a long, hard look at my plot and realised it's been used a million times before. Should I bother continuing?**

A *The problem with an outline – any outline – is that its brevity makes it look like any number of previously written books. But if you know your characters intimately then the outline transforms into a unique story the moment you start writing. Stay true to your characters, their strengths and individuality.*

35

The Big Bang

When it comes to children's books you have to make a good impression in your first paragraph. If you don't, your readers will never make it past page one.

If you've ever spent time around children then you'll know just how impatient they can be. If something doesn't appeal to them straight away then chances are it never will.

Because of this, you have to grab a reader with the very first words of your book, and the best way to do this is to begin with an action scene.

ACTION STATIONS!

Never start a novel by introducing information about your characters – describing who they are, where they live or what they like. This is a static opening with about as much pulling power as a warthog in a disco. Always begin with what is known as a 'crash start', a scene in which something dramatic is happening. Think about any good action film, and the way that they often start with a character smack in the middle of a crisis. You don't know who this person is yet, but you are so caught up in the action and the excitement of the situation that you are prepared to wait to find out.

Here's an idea for you... **Write down several different ideas for the opening chapter of a novel – they can be anything. Now, practise writing the opening few paragraphs for each idea, trying to start each one with a dramatic hook. Put your characters in a sticky situation of some kind and watch them fight their way out of it. Focus on the action, the thrill of the moment. You don't have to write much and don't worry about making them perfect. It's a great way to experiment with different beginnings to work out what gives the biggest bang.**

Children's books work in the same way. Plunged right into the middle of an action scene a reader will be gripped, and will want to read on to discover how the situation resolves itself and to find out more about the people involved in the action. And the situation doesn't have to be explosive – action can include an argument in the home, a child realising he is lost, an incident of bullying at school, even an interesting conversation. If you plunge a reader into the centre of any of these events, emphasising the sense of drama, excitement and intrigue, they will continue reading. You can then go on to introduce the characters properly in the next few pages or the next chapter, as the reader will be too hooked to mind the change in pace.

TIME TRAVEL

If your plot centres on a single event which doesn't happen until later on, then you should still start with a crash bang. Think about opening the book with a flash-forward to the event – showing an alien invasion in full swing or a volcanic eruption about to engulf a small town. Pick out the most exciting details and end the chapter on a cliffhanger, before starting the book properly in chapter two, some time before the climactic event takes place. Alternatively, show your hero involved in an unrelated action scene – perhaps a teenage detective fighting for his life on a previous case. Although unconnected to the main plot, the excitement of the scene hooks the reader and promises more of the same to follow.

If you're not sure where to go from here then find your way with IDEA 33, *The Magnificent Seven.*

Try another idea...

You can also use a flashback, showing a dramatic scene from hundreds of years ago which effects the novel's plot – a black magic ceremony, perhaps, designed to awaken some terrible evil in the future. Getting action into the first few paragraphs is the most important thing, and don't worry about making everything crystal clear – the sense of mystery at not knowing exactly who everybody is helps grip the reader further.

ALL CHANGE

'I try to create sympathy for my characters, then turn the monsters loose.'
STEPHEN KING

Defining idea...

Don't start your book with a random incident, make sure it's tied in with the overall plot.
Begin at a moment of change or crisis in the life of your main character, anything that will have consequences which propel the story onwards. In short, start on a day that is different.

'We read five words on the first page of a really good novel and we begin to forget that we are reading printed words on a page; we begin to see images.'
JOHN GARDNER

Defining idea...

155

How did it go?

Q   I'm finding it difficult to launch into an action scene without introducing my characters. What should I do?

A   *If you really are struggling to kick-start the book with some action, and feel like you need to set the scene and establish the characters first, then do it. Start by introducing your protagonists, getting the ball rolling, and carry on until you reach a scene with action. When you're there, make this the starting point and shift the introductions to the next chapter. It may need some serious polishing to make sense, but it will be a better story.*

Q   It's impossible to start this idea for a novel with an action scene, is there any way to use another technique and still hook the reader?

A   *If you're not starting with an action scene it isn't the end of the world, just make sure you hint that there will be action soon. Providing a promise of action – 'When Will woke to the sound of demolition trucks outside his window he knew today was going to be different' – can be just as effective a hook as action itself. Action can simply be movement.*

Q   Can I use something other than action?

A   *Try opening with dialogue. Speech acts in the same way as action, hooking a reader and introducing a character. Don't use a flat, boring statement, however, make it something dynamic and exciting. If you're writing in the first person, some internal speech will work just as well:* I can tell you the exact moment my life went to hell.

36

The middle man

A great plot is all very well, but always remember that even if you know where events are leading, readers like to be kept in suspense.

Keep their blood pressure permanently high through the middle of your book by creating questions and delaying answers.

Making a book 'unputdownable' is all about keeping your readers hooked. If you can get them guessing right from the start then you've got them for the rest of the book, and they'll plough through a thousand pages or more to find out the answers.

The biggest question you will pose when writing your book is the one established at the beginning – the initiating event – and which most likely isn't resolved until the end. But readers aren't simply looking for a final payoff; if they were then all stories would simply be two pages long. Yes, they want to get to the end of the novel as quickly as possible, but they want to feel as though they've been on a journey by the time they get there.

Here's an idea for you... **Try visualising your plot line as a blueprint for a roller coaster. Think about incidents you could build into the story that readers will want to see resolved. Each time your characters meet a new obstacle and a question is raised, draw an uphill track. When the challenge is resolved and the question answered, create the drop. If the line is too flat you need to create more questions; if it would make a stunt pilot hurl you might be overdoing it!**

UNPUTDOWNABLE

Keeping your readers engaged in the middle of your book is all about sustaining the excitement of the opening and keeping the flow going as you gradually build towards the climax. You must create difficulties and obstacles for your characters that become increasingly risky or dangerous, with their responses determining the path they follow in relation to the main plot.

These secondary problems can be seen at their simplest in picture books, where the main character often faces a number of smaller setbacks as the story develops, or starts to think that the quest is becoming ever more difficult. These problems don't always occur on every page, but when they do present themselves they help increase the stakes.

Take a story about a duckling who is trying to find her way home. A short way into the story she may meet a fox who appears to be friendly, but who has a mean glint in his eye. If the duckling eventually loses the fox, she might then meet a cat, and so on. The greatest question remains: will the duckling make it home? The secondary challenges sustain the drama and keep the reader turning the pages.

LEAVE THEM HANGING

In novels, the process works in exactly the same way, albeit with more complex problems and solutions. Create challenges for your characters that become increasingly dramatic as the plot progresses. Don't just throw any old setback at them – make sure that these minor incidents are tied in to the main story otherwise they will seem artificial. Each one of these obstacles will be a question raised, creating uncertainty. If they become harder each time, or if your characters have more to lose than they did with the previous challenge, then this suspense will grip a reader more powerfully with each incident.

The longer you hold back the answer to each problem, the greater the suspense. And one of the best ways of getting readers to stay up all night reading is to leave the question unanswered at the end of each chapter, or to provide a solution to one question but create another before breaking away. Readers will often be so desperate to find out how the characters face up to this new hurdle that they'll just start the next chapter.

The middle of the book can be a difficult beast to keep under control, but it helps if you use an outline. Check out IDEA 34, *Are we there yet?*.

Try another idea...

'I believe that good questions are more important than answers, and the best children's books ask questions, and make the readers ask questions. And every new question is going to disturb someone's universe.'
MADELEINE L'ENGLE

Defining idea...

Each challenge should also shape your characters. Somewhere between each uncertainty and each resolution your heroes need to grow – emotionally and physically – so that when they finally arrive at the climax of your story they can meet it as stronger individuals than they were at the beginning. They will only do this if their responses to each challenge are genuine. If they don't change and evolve with each problem then their ultimate victory is in danger of appearing shallow and meaningless.

Q   **I'm having trouble ending my chapters on cliffhangers – I just keep writing! Is there an easy way to know when to cut off?**

A   *The best place to end a chapter is at the moment of greatest danger, or with a terrible revelation. If you don't know where to end, then don't! Keep writing, then read back over the chapter and work out the most dramatic place to cut. The rest can be used in the next chapter.*

Q   **Some of my secondary problems overlap. Any suggestions?**

A   *Usually it's best if you keep them separate. Each scene should only have one problem or setback, and it should be resolved relatively quickly to keep up the momentum. Instead of dragging one problem out and risking losing the suspense, try ending it and creating a new one immediately.*

Q   **Um... I'm not quite sure what you mean by minor setbacks and obstacles. Can you provide a few examples?**

A   *Sure. Basically they should be related to the plot of the story but they shouldn't be the main incident itself – in other words if your characters solve the secondary problem they shouldn't be left with nothing to do. Minor setbacks can include the weather, illness, something going wrong with a piece of machinery, a surprise announcement, a minor accident or even the death of a minor character. Each one should drive the plot forward and help your characters evolve.*

How did it go?

161

THE END.

37

It's all over!

When you're entering the home straight it's tempting to relax, but the ending of your book is the most important part – it must tie up the plot in an exciting way.

How many times have you been utterly engrossed in a book — or film, for that matter — only to feel robbed because of a rubbish ending?

When you invest time and emotion in a story and its characters you expect a satisfying conclusion, and if you don't get it, then no matter how good the rest of the experience was, the whole thing is ruined.

The ending of the book is the place where the suspense built up throughout your story reaches its greatest point, where your heroes face their biggest challenge, make their most stunning discovery and either achieve their goals or fail, but learn something valuable as a result.

Here's an idea for you...

Pick one of your favourite books, ideally aimed at the age range you are writing for, and reread it. When you get to the final climax, though, stop. Try and write the ending yourself, matching the tone of the rest of the book and making it as dramatic as possible. You can either keep the events of the climax the same or change them, it's up to you.

MOMENT OF TRUTH

You may already know what happens at the end of your book, or you may be waiting to see where your characters lead you. But there are certain things that children expect when they reach the climax of a story.

The characters should reach a point where their goals are finally in reach, or where the threat is almost upon them, where they face a real win or lose situation. This is always tied in to the plot of your novel – if it has focused on people trying to stage a school play then it is the night of the performance. If it's a picture book about a child who has lost a toy then it should seem as though it will never be found.

Never give your characters an easy ride towards the end. The climax of your story should be the point of greatest tension, and readers really shouldn't know whether your heroes will be successful or not. Help raise the tension by building in a scene where it really looks like they will fail, moments before they succeed. Having your characters so close to catastrophe will make their victory so much more rewarding.

HAPPILY EVER AFTER

Of course, you might not be planning on letting your characters achieve their goals at all. But be careful. Children, younger ones especially, like to see someone succeed. They like to feel that despite all the odds being against them, and the terrible danger, the hero has pulled through and everything is well.

This doesn't mean that a character always has to be victorious. Not all the goals that children have are achievable – or should be achieved – and it could even be considered cruel if you implied that they were. But if somebody is unsuccessful then they should still have learned something from the experience, and emerge as a stronger, better person. Even if they have lost, or backed down, they must still be able to triumph in some way – even if it is simply to lose magnanimously. If they meet complete and utter failure at the end then your book will be a huge disappointment.

Writing 'The End' doesn't mean the hard work's over. Find a red pen and read IDEA 46, *Nip / Tuck.*

Try another idea…

CASE CLOSED

In the climax, your writing has to be at its best. Keep your sentences short to help propel the action along, cut anything that slows down the pace (excess description or any unnecessary adverbs and adjectives), use strong verbs and make sure that the action is easy to follow. If kids have to read a sentence twice because it isn't clear then the pace can be ruined.

Be sure to end in a way that feels realistic in relation to the rest of the book – in other words, don't finish a funny book with a murder. The most important thing is that the climax has to provide closure. While adults are happy to torture themselves with open-ended stories, kids demand more care and attention. Whatever happens, the plot needs to be resolved.

'I try to have reasonably happy endings because I would hate any child to be cast down in gloom and despair; I want to show them they can find a way out of it.'
JACQUELINE WILSON

Defining idea…

How did
it go?

Q I've finished the dramatic climax of my book but it feels weird to stop here. Is it a good idea to add a final scene to let readers relax a little?

A *Definitely – if you stop too soon then readers might feel short-changed. They've been holding their breath through the action of the climax, so add a short, gentle final scene where the heroes can collect themselves and take stock. Don't make them openly discuss the lessons learned or victories achieved throughout the story, though, or make it too long – it would be an anticlimax.*

Q I can't think of a good way to finish. Are there any stock endings I can borrow?

A *Well, there's 'happily ever after', obviously, where everything turns out fine. A variation is the 'safely back home' ending, where the hero returns from a quest (internal or external) to find home just as it was before. Some endings imply that a new adventure is about to start, and are often used for sequels. You could even use an ending that seems sad, but which promises a new adventure.*

Q I was so excited that I wrote the ending hurriedly and it's lacking something. Any suggestions?

A *There's nothing wrong with writing in a white-hot passion as you reach the climax, but don't rush it by neglecting the action, skipping over the final scenes and squashing everything into a couple of paragraphs.*

38

Tearing down the house

Creating a realistic setting is vital if you want your readers to know where they are. In your book you can decide on the layout of the entire world!

Think of your favourite characters and the chances are their surroundings will appear with them — Harry Potter in Hogwarts, Winnie the Pooh in the Hundred Acre Wood...

The setting of your book may seem far less important than the people and events that populate it. But the imaginative world in which your drama unfolds is part of what makes a character come alive on the page. Think about a stage play – if the scenery appears shoddy and poorly made, then the cast isn't going to seem real either.

WALKING THE LINE

There's a fine line between interior design that's tasteful and decoration that's ridiculously over the top. Well, this line also exists in fiction. It's tempting to go overboard when you're describing a place – detailing every species of plant in the flowerbeds or the exact number of stripes on the garish wallpaper. But if you try to

Here's an idea for you...

This exercise works best with a character from your own writing who you've been working on for a while, one you know pretty well. Start by writing a short sketch placing this character inside your own home, concentrating on the things she'd pick up on about her new surroundings and the assumptions she'd make about the way you live. Next, transport her to a new location, something completely different. What are the first things she notices about this new place?

outline everything then, ironically, you're pushing people away, not drawing them in. Instead of feeling immersed in your imaginative realm, readers will be overloaded with pointless information and will return their attention to the real world. On the other side of the line, there is also a danger of not including enough clues to remind readers where they are, an error which also forces them to drift away.

ON THE BEACH

The trick is to tread lightly, and keep it personal. In other words, avoid unspecific clichés such as 'It was a bright, sunny day on the beach'. Everybody knows what the beach looks like, but when we are presented with a general, stock description like this all we get is a fuzzy and imprecise mental image. The fact is that people don't necessarily notice the grand picture first off, and your characters won't either.

In order to bring a scene to life, focus on the details that your characters would notice first, the aspects of the setting that are important to them. Think about the first things *you* are aware of when you visit a new place: the sun on your face, sand crumbling between your toes, the distant call of seagulls and the gentle roar of the sea. Realistic characters will register the same sorts of specific details, and by describing a select few of these evocative descriptions not only will you conjure a believable world in a very short space, but you'll also be revealing your characters' emotional engagement to their surroundings, illuminating more about them and the way they view the world.

Learn what makes a location's atmosphere unique. See the world from a new perspective in IDEA 39, *Open your eyes.*

Try another idea...

JOIN THE DOTS

Another important thing to remember when setting the scene is that description is most effective when it is active. Instead of reeling off several sentences of minute detail, mix it with action. For example, don't waste time providing information about everybody on the beach, simply state something like 'Lucy weaved her way around the throng of scantily dressed tourists who were gently frying in the sun'.

Likewise, describe objects only when they have a use – there's no need to point out that there's a kettle in a kitchen unless a character is making tea. You may worry that unless you describe everything your readers may not picture it exactly the way you do, but this is the whole point of fiction! All children have vivid imaginations, and don't want to be told exactly how to see the world. If you provide the right sensory hints, if you include the essentials and keep the setting personal, then they'll join the dots and your world will take on a new life in their minds, becoming unforgettable because it's as much their creation as yours.

'What a miracle it is that out of these small, flat, rigid squares of paper unfolds world after world after world, worlds that sing to you, comfort and quiet and excite you.'
ANNE LAMOTT, US author

Defining idea...

How did it go?

Q **I'm having trouble describing a character in my own home, let alone in an exotic location. Should I give up?**

A *No – start by looking at your home in a new light. Describe it as if you'd never been there before. Record the smallest details, and remember that you've got five senses. The chances are you're so familiar with the place that you never really look at it, so try and see it with a newcomer's curiosity. You'll find it much easier to identify the details that your character will pick up on.*

Q **I'm also having trouble picking specific details. Is it OK to start a scene by saying 'It was a dark and stormy night'?**

A *Well, it's OK, it just isn't great. If you're starting a scene in a storm then don't try and sum it up in a cliché, write it from your character's point of view. Show her coming out of her house, the sleet pounding her skin, the wind tying her hair in knots. Describing anything from your character's point of view (you can explore her thoughts using a third-person narrator) will always be far more powerful and evocative.*

Q **Even when I'm picking specific details things seem a bit vague. Are there any other ways to tighten things up?**

A *Lack of definition in a description can have this effect. Be specific – don't just write 'tree', give it its proper name: 'oak' or 'elm'. It helps define the scene and gives you a greater appearance of authority.*

39

Open your eyes

Good description isn't just about writing well, it's also about *seeing* well. Every place on earth (and off) has a unique atmosphere.

If you can tune into this then you're well on your way to creating a setting that truly comes to life.

You're only really successful as a writer if you've made your readers feel as though they've visited the world of your book personally by the time they turn the last page, and if part of them wishes that this fictional realm was real. The key to evoking these feelings is simply opening your eyes.

ONE OF A KIND

Whatever the location, it has a unique atmosphere, created by countless variables. If you can pin down the factors that give a place its own particular atmosphere then you'll be able to turn it into a rich, three-dimensional, multi-sensory setting on the page. Whether you're setting your book in your own back yard or the lower decks of a star cruiser, the key to capturing this atmosphere is by learning to describe the

Here's an idea for you...

Visit one of your favourite places. Sit down somewhere out of the way, where you won't be disturbed. Spend a couple of hours observing the location and making notes, looking for the tiny details that make the place special, the ones you might never have noticed before – and use all your senses. Before long you'll have created a cumulative build-up of detail that you can use in your writing.

world around you. But this isn't as easy as it sounds. It's all very well opening your eyes and *looking* around, but there is a big difference between this and *seeing* what's there. How well could you describe the room you're in now if you closed your eyes? Could you recreate the small details in your imagination? What about the route you take to work, can you see it in your mind's eye?

A STRANGER CALLS

The chances are you'll have a vague impression of the room and the route, but the vital details will be missing (unless you've got a photographic memory). We all take our surroundings for granted, our brains blank out the little things because they have no direct relevance to the way we live our lives. But these tiny details may be the difference between a setting that's bland and nondescript, and one that pulls readers in even after they've finished the book.

The trick to spotting details like this is to overcome the temporary blindness. In order to ensure that your readers can picture a scene as clearly as you do, it's essential that you approach it from the same way they do: from outside. Everywhere you go, imagine it was the first time you'd been there. Note all the tiny details and ask yourself what these minute visual clues represent. But don't just use the one sense. How does the location smell? What can you hear? Is it a relaxing place or does it make you feel cramped and stressed? Try and describe the atmosphere of the room or the space, and what it says about whoever lives there (even if that person is you).

If you need to explore foreign lands or fantasy worlds, get some travel tips at IDEA 10, Bless you!.

Try another idea...

THE MIND'S EYE

You may be wondering about how counting the dustballs under your sofa will help you bring a scene to life on the page, but it should become clear next time you sit down to write. What you're doing is learning which details are the ones which stand out, which a character would notice and which can be used to recreate the essence of the location in your book. If you've only a vague picture of a setting in your mind then your description of it will be unexciting.

It's just the same if you're writing about imaginary places, which is most likely. If you come to understand the details that make up a familiar place then you'll know what to look for when you enter a fictional world. You'll be able to spot the same kinds of sights, you'll be assaulted by the same array of sounds and smells and tastes – as if you were actually there. You'll be able to visualise a living, breathing location rather than just a fuzzy impression, and as a result you'll know exactly how to transpose this realm into your writing.

'The author must know his countryside, whether real or imagined, like his hand.'
ROBERT LOUIS STEVENSON

Defining idea...

How did it go?

Q **I've filled pages of my notebook with minute descriptions, but when I try and fit them into my writing it seems OTT. Am I doing something wrong?**

A *You don't have to use everything. Pinpoint what it is about a place that makes it special, which creates its unique atmosphere. Leave your notes for a day or two then come back to them, and pick out a handful that best capture its essence; this leads to a much more realistic description than a long list of details.*

Q **I have to pause to think of good words when I'm in the middle of writing descriptive scenes. Is there a good way to have a stash ready to use?**

A *Er... Yes, why don't you compile a stash of suitable words? If you're about to write a scene with a rocket taking off, make a list of different words which convey the heat, the noise, the excitement, the fear. Then you can just pick a suitable word without having to pause for thought.*

Q **I'm trying to see the detail in my imaginary setting but I'm finding it hard to focus! Are there any good ways to know which details to look for?**

A *When you're writing a book you shouldn't create homes for your characters which they obviously aren't suited to. If you're struggling to see the details in a scene then ask your characters what kinds of things they'd have, and what details are important to them. As well as helping you create a realistic setting, this will also help you delve more deeply into a character's personality.*

40

Drool-proof books

Writing books for babies and very young children is nothing like stealing candy from, well, a baby.

You've got to find the right words and pictures to keep your audience engaged.

If you want to write books for the 'chew-it-and-see' age group then it's all about making them enjoyable for both infant and reader – and giving a child a valuable head start in learning to learn.

Let's be honest, it doesn't take a masterful wordsmith to add the word 'tree' to an illustration of a tree. Because of this, most books for babies are commissioned and written by staff inside a publishing company. If you want to find a publisher, then you have to suggest something strikingly new.

BEING BABY

At their simplest, books for babies are bath-time books, board books and cloth books, designed to engender a love of books in children who don't yet understand what stories or even words are. Thinking of ideas for this age range is a huge creative challenge because you have to consider the entire format of the book – the words themselves, if there are any, take a back seat to the illustrations and even the shape of the book.

Here's an idea for you... **Think of something that would be familiar to a baby or young child – having a bath, eating breakfast – and plan a wordless story around it. Think about typical, or unusual, things that could happen and visualise them as they would appear on each page. Next, think about which words you would add to each illustration – no more than four or five per page. Lastly, is there any way you could change the shape or feel of your book to better appeal to babies?**

When looking for ideas, think about how a baby can interact with a book. If you're writing about animals, plan a cloth book with soft fabrics that can be stroked, for instance. Picture books can be cut into any shape imaginable, or printed on practically anything, so expand your imagination and think of something completely unique which is inventive and fun.

If you've got an idea for a story, try and imagine how the shape and design of the book could reflect the theme. Thing big, think expansively! Eric Carle's much-loved story *The Very Hungry Caterpillar* is made even more entertaining because of the holes cut into the pages – as if chewed out by the title character. Don't shy away from suggesting new ideas to a publisher. If Dorothy Kunhardt hadn't approached Golden Books with the idea for *Pat the Bunny* then the 'touch and feel' book may never have been invented, and your idea may be the next big thing.

KNOW YOUR READERS

It also pays to look closely at the people you are writing for. Some people say that babies can make out images much more clearly when they are simply black and white. If you create or suggest monotone illustrations to enable a child to focus on the story then a publisher will know you've done your research. Alternatively, suggest books that make sounds – a sense that is more developed in a new baby. Also think about ones that will fit into baby hands, or designs that will enable babies to turn the pages themselves – important for teaching them how books work and ensuring that they can look at yours when their parents are too busy.

If your idea is looking too sophisticated for babies maybe you should turn it into a picture book. Check out IDEA 41, *Seeing the whole picture*, for where to start.

Try another idea...

WORDLESS WONDERS

Many baby books have a handful of words, while some have none at all. Just because there aren't many, or any, words, however, doesn't mean that a book isn't written. Helen Oxenbury's *Dressing* is the perfect example of a wordless story which focuses on a toddler dealing with the extremely difficult job of getting dressed. If you're planning a wordless book then think hard about your chosen subject and how it will be represented by the illustrations. An adult will still try and 'read' the story, so make sure there is enough substance to allow plenty of talk.

If you are using words, then make sure that they sound fun. Babies and young children won't understand all the words you use, but they will respond to the sound they make. Alliteration (such as 'splish splash') and onomatopoeia are always recommended because they are great to say and to hear, and help babies develop an ear for language.

'A new baby is like the beginning of all things – wonder, hope, a dream, of possibilities.'
EDNA LE SHAN, US author

Defining idea...

How did it go? **Q   I know babies are curious about everything, so should I plan some complex and detailed pictures for every page?**

A   *Yes, babies are curious, but they can't comprehend complicated pictures. Make sure your pictures are large, simple and uncluttered. Avoid the kind of crowded images you'd see in a picture book – these are great for six-year-olds but will mean nothing to a baby. Instead, have bold pictures of everyday objects and, best of all, of faces. And don't just use pictures, incorporate mirrors or slots for photos into your book, enabling babies to look at themselves and their loved ones while reading.*

Q   I've got an idea that's a bit too complex for babies, and a bit too simplistic for the picture book market. How do I go about pitching a book at toddlers?

A   *Children who're walking the walk and talking the talk have different needs to babies who're flat out on their backs all day. Books for toddlers are still likely to get chewed up and spat out, and they still need to be every bit as colourful, textured or noisy as baby books. But they're also stepping stones on the way to 'proper' story books and a great opportunity to help shape young minds. These books should be a rich source of basic vocabulary disguised as fun, fun, fun. You needn't be afraid of repeating yourself. In fact, it's best if you do!*

41
Seeing the whole picture

Picture books are most children's first glance at the world of literature. So you're not just creating a fun book, but shaping a child's view of the world.

The thought of starting a picture book can be quite daunting to new writers, especially when it comes to finding a good idea.

A picture book uses the same essential components as a novel – characters readers and listeners identify with and a plot in which those characters face some kind of conflict. As with all stories, it's the challenges that characters face and the ways they try to overcome them which make readers want to turn page after page. Don't assume that you can get away with a half-baked story or two-dimensional characters.

IDEAS...

Because children are relatively new to the world, everything can be exciting. Think back to when you were a child, about what things fascinated you or scared you, and what questions you relentlessly asked your beleaguered parents. I was fascinated by what could possibly be in the shed in the garden, because I wasn't allowed inside. It turned out to be full of rusty tools, but that isn't the point – these childhood ideas can be the perfect starting place, allowing you to reach inside your own imagination.

Here's an idea for you...

If you've got an idea for a picture book but are not quite sure how to develop it, then try and pin down its theme. What message are you trying to create? An idea can evolve in an infinite number of ways depending on the theme you choose, and by playing around with the fundamental message you can discover the most interesting way to develop it on the page. Just always remember that themes must be shown, not told.

VERSUS THEMES

While thinking about your idea, you should also think about the theme. They might seem like the same thing, but they're not – the idea for your book may be a puppy who is afraid of everything, but the theme could be that although you start off small and helpless, you soon grow into a strong, confident person who isn't scared of anything. Knowing your theme can help you build and develop an idea because the theme is like the cement that keeps a story together. Ask yourself, when writing, if every page contributes to the theme. If a page or section of the book doesn't illustrate this essence, then ask yourself if you really need it.

Themes should never be explicitly told, they should be shown through the characters' feelings and actions. This is more important with picture books than any other form of fiction, because it helps keep them fresh even when they are read repeatedly. If you simply state your theme then the book can only be read one way, and children won't be able to interpret it for themselves. If it is just implied, however, then there will be depth and substance, and something new to take away every time it is read.

KEEP IT REAL

Of course, the most important aspect of a picture book, as with a novel, is your characters. Children want to fall in love with the main character, and to do this they have to empathise, to feel as though they themselves are part of the adventure. Pick a character a child will identify with. This usually means writing about a child but it can be an animal – or even an adult, but one with a childlike sense of fun and adventure.

Most importantly, this character has to face the same conflicts as those a child will be confronted with – for example, a child won't necessarily know what a war is but he might have heard adults arguing. If you create a realistic problem, and a character responds to it in a believable way, then there will be an underlying emotional truth which will entertain as well as help kids cope with their own difficulties. By the end of the book your character will have grown or learned a lesson which makes him stronger. Always leave your readers feeling safe and happy, not just for their own peace of mind but because it is the satisfying ending of a book that makes a child want to read it over and over.

You still need to know everything about your main character. Read IDEA 25, *I want to be a real boy!*.

Try another idea...

'**We can get away with things in children's books that nobody in the adult world ever can because the assumption is that the audience is too innocent to pick it up. And in truth they're the only audience that does pick it up.**'
MAURICE SENDAK

Defining idea...

How did it go?

Q   Do I need to plan out a picture book using an outline, or can I just wing it?

A   *It's still useful to make a rough plan. Write down the name of your character, his problems or goals, the various setbacks he meets in the course of the story and how he'll have changed by the end. If you're not sure about the various minor conflicts that will impede his journey then try this: on the left hand side of a sheet of paper write the ways that he will try to achieve his main goal, then on the other side of the paper list at least one complication that could result from each action. Brainstorm possible scenarios resulting from each item. You won't use everything, but it will create a useful list of possible complications that can develop the plot.*

Q   Is there something more basic I can do?

A   *Try and describe the idea for your book in one sentence. If you can't, then the chances are it's too long or too complex.*

Q   I've thought of a theme but I'm finding it hard to make my characters do as they're told. They seem a little wooden. Why?

A   *Just because you've thought of a plot based on your theme doesn't mean your story must follow it exactly. Use it as a starting point but let your characters act naturally and allow them to lead the way. You may have to change the theme, but this will make a far better book.*

42

A piece of string

Deciding how long to make a picture book is tricky – too long and readers will get bored before the end, too short and they'll still be hungry for more.

Writers generally aren't the most disciplined of people, especially when it comes to reining in their prose. When it comes to picture books this can be a nightmare.

LUCKY NUMBER THIRTY-TWO

Believe it or not, standard picture books all have exactly the same number of pages – a total of thirty-two. This has nothing to do with how long kids like their books, or how much time parents have at night to read a story, but with the printing process. It may seem unfair to have something so banal as this dominate your work of art, but the sad truth is that these colourful books are extremely expensive to print, and if they're longer than thirty-two pages the cost becomes astronomical.

And you don't even get all of those pages! Look at any picture book and you'll see that the first double page spread, and the last, are given up to endpapers (which

Here's an idea for you... **Don't start writing a picture book like you would any other story. Make up a dummy book using sixteen pages of blank paper, landscape rather than portrait, with a line drawn down the centre of each to show where the gutter lies. Space out your story on each page as you visualise it in the finished book, writing it by hand and adding sketches and doodles. This gives you a much better idea of the finished book and stops you overwriting.**

rarely contribute to the story), while the second is lost to the publisher's information (usually on page three) and the title page next to it. This leaves you with a measly twelve double page spreads, or twenty-four single pages.

LITTLE HORSE

When I was writing my first picture book, *Little Horse*, I had no idea of the rules. I set off to write a short book, but my verbal diarrhoea kicked in and it ended up being forty-two pages long, with over 1,500 words. Of course, I didn't care – I just sent it off to publisher after publisher. Each time it came back without so much as an editor's note, just a standard 'thanks but no thanks' slip.

In desperation I sat down and tried to work out what was different about the books already on the market, and several sleepless, coffee-fuelled days later I eventually noticed that they all shared the same page length – with no exceptions. I unchained my internal editor and made *Little Horse* even littler, so that it would fit comfortably into twelve double page spreads. The next publisher I sent it to showed an interest.

WHAT'S THE BIG IDEA?

Rules are made to be broken, but unless your
name is Maurice Sendak don't try and bend
these. Publishers just won't give you more than thirty-two pages, especially if it's
your first book. But don't think of this restriction as a curse, think of it as a blessing.
Writing to a strict format like this can actually be beneficial to the story you are
telling, helping you to trim off excess material and create a more controlled, more
masterful work of art.

And one of the most important things to remember when writing picture books is
not to think of the text as a very short story, but as a poem. Like poetry, a picture
book must focus on one simple idea – even if
the idea itself encompasses bigger things. For
example a four-year-old child may not
understand animal rights, but she will
understand that it is cruel to kick a cat.

Also in common with poetry, the text has to be
short to help keep a child's attention – every
word must be perfect simply because there are
so few of them. You have to use the best words in the best order, as Coleridge defined
poetry. When writing, ask yourself if each word expresses your idea as richly and
clearly as possible, and if it doesn't then ruthlessly delete it. If you've never written
poetry before, don't panic – I'm not saying you have to write in rhyming couplets. But
working on a picture book like this will ensure that your story doesn't grow too long
and too complex – the one thing guaranteed to make a publisher say no.

**Get the picture about
illustrators in IDEA 43, _Worth a
thousand words_.**

Try another idea...

**'If kids like a picture book,
they're going to read it at
least fifty times. Read
anything that often, and even
minor imperfections start to
feel like gravel in the bed.'**
MARK HADDON

Defining idea...

How did
it go?

Q   It's no use, I just can't trim down my story to fit into thirty-two pages! What now?

A   *Ask yourself if it would really be best as a picture book, or if it would be better aimed at older kids. A short chapter book for children just learning to read might be a better option, with more text and fewer illustrations. If you've already finished a book and it's too long, then trying to prune down an overlong picture book isn't a bad thing anyway. Imagine you were a parent reading the book every night for a year, and cut out anything that gets annoying. Keep the original, though!*

Q   I'm struggling with the whole poetry thing, any suggestions?

A   *All I'm saying is that you have to ensure that every word is a gem. Pick one of your favourite fairy tales or short children's stories, then try and rewrite it as a picture book. This should help you get a better sense of the importance of every single word.*

Q   I'm finding it difficult to plan out my story in such a short amount of space. Do I need a shoehorn?

A   *Fitting everything in is one of the biggest challenges of writing a picture book, and one of the main reasons why it's harder than it looks. Generally, the middle should be the longest part, with around eight spreads, while the beginning and the end could have two spreads each.*

43

Worth a thousand words

Creating a picture book is double trouble – getting the words down on the page is only half the task.

Your art skills may be limited, but there are a few things worth remembering if you want your work to be a masterpiece.

There's no other way of saying it – most picture books rely as much on their illustrations as they do on their text. This is fine if your name is Picasso, but for the rest of us this can cause problems. Despite this, however, it's vital to be able to draw something if you want your picture book to be your vision.

LOSING CONTROL

Don't worry, I'm not suggesting that you illustrate your book yourself. Apart from a few lucky buggers who are extremely talented at both writing and illustrating – Maurice Sendak, Oliver Jeffers, Lauren Child – the rest of us will be relying on somebody else to turn our ideas into big, beautiful images on the page. This can be a daunting thought.

Here's an idea for you... **Get into the habit of sketching every time you write – either using your notebook or keeping a separate illustration journal. Visualise your characters and their settings, focusing on their expressions and poses. Draw plans of each page of your book, trying out different designs and layouts. These drawings are for your eyes only but they will help you build up a detailed visual picture of your world, enabling you to keep control when somebody else is illustrating.**

What makes things infinitely worse is that in most circumstances a publisher will pick an illustrator they think best suits your work. Although they will never admit it, it all comes down to control – a publisher is always concerned about losing artistic control of a project, which is more likely to happen if an author and an illustrator work together. But it isn't all bad news – you'll always have some say in who gets to illustrate your work, and a collaboration with a complete stranger can help you see your story in a completely new light.

PICTURE PERFECT

Because you won't be the one in charge of the inkpot and paintbrushes, it's vitally important that you think visually when writing. Remember, anything that appears on the page as a picture doesn't have to form part of the text, so you don't have to waste valuable words describing it. Just look at the start of *Where the Wild Things Are*. According to the text, Max simply 'made mischief of one kind and another', but the glorious illustrations show him hammering a nail into the wall, hanging up his toy and chasing the dog with a fork.

Try covering up the pictures and just reading the text. The book simply doesn't work. Now cover up the text and see if you can follow the story using only the illustrations. Although something is missing, the plot is still relatively easy to follow and each character's expressions and actions are clearly visible. In good picture books, the pictures can tell the story on their own, which is why it is essential that you attempt to sketch them out before you send your book to a publisher.

If you're looking for ways to make your picture book fun then start a party at IDEA 44, *Play time*, and invite everyone to join in.

Try another idea...

BETWEEN THE LINES

Don't just think about the main illustrations, try and incorporate a subtext into your sketches. Most successful picture books have an added dimension that runs in parallel with the main story, and this is usually told solely through images. Think about a running theme that you could add to every page – a minor character such as a mouse who is trying to negotiate a hunk of cheese through a hole in the wall, perhaps. Although this theme would only be subtly added to the corner of each page, it will provide an added dimension to the text. Likewise, think of visual jokes that you can add to each illustration, like those used by the Ahlbergs. If a book is going to be read every single night, then these added touches will keep children and parents entertained.

'At first, I see pictures of a story in my mind. Then creating the story comes from asking questions of myself. I guess you might call it the 'what if, what then' approach to writing and illustration.'
CHRIS VAN ALLSBURG, US author and illustrator

Defining idea...

How did it go? **Q** **When I think about my picture I book I really want it to look like the classics. Will I be able to request an illustrator who uses that particular style?**

A *Before you set your mind on a certain 'look', think long and hard about what it says about the book. Illustration fashions change, and children used to the bright, innovative designs of modern picture books (like the* Charlie and Lola *series) may not get excited about something that looks like it's thirty years old. Done well, a classic look can strike the right tone for a particular kind of book, but the chances are a publisher will be more concerned with appealing to a modern audience and will ask for something fresh.*

Q **If pictures can tell the story then why should I bother with words?**

A *Pictures show each segment of a story, and a child can leap from one to the next to work out what is going on. But no matter how full of life and action they are, illustrations are static. They capture the vibrancy and excitement of a particular moment, but they need your words in order to link each part of the whole and drive the story forwards. Think of it as looking at the frames from a movie – you need movement to turn the frozen pictures into a film. The words of a picture book let a reader know how they get from one picture to the next, providing a sense of motion that brings the story to life.*

44

Play time

One of the most common reasons for very young children to be bored with picture books is because they don't feel part of the story.

So if you want to ensure that children fall in love with your story, invite them to join in.

The aim of any picture book is to entrance its readers, and while any story can be entertaining if written well, only those which invite children to step into the story and participate will truly engage their readers and listeners. Of course, the easy way to do this is to create an interactive book – with pop-ups, flaps or 'touch and feel' surfaces – but even those books with no novelty design should pull children into the story by encouraging them to play.

WORD GAMES

A great way to get young children to join in is to let them finish your rhymes. Although writing in rhyme is far harder than working with prose – publishers hold you to the very highest standards, and won't tolerate anything but a strong, consistent meter and a full, true rhyme – it can be the perfect way to involve your readers in the story. Try placing the last line of each rhyme on a different page,

Here's an idea for you... **If you're having trouble finding the right spark, then try using one of these methods. Don't write a story which uses all of them, but good use of one of these techniques can certainly add colour and flavour to a book. More importantly, if you use a playful idea as a starting point you may find it triggers new ideas in your head, allowing you to set off in an entirely new direction.**

allowing young children to guess what is coming and shout out the word they think finishes the rhyme. If you adopt this approach, however, make sure you give plenty of clues as to what the answer is, so as not to confuse readers. Whatever you do, don't leave yourself open to undesirable answers – it's best to avoid the word 'duck' altogether.

Another excellent way to encourage a reader to join in at various points throughout the book is to include refrains in the story, elements or choruses which are repeated at regular intervals. This can work either with prose or with verse – or a combination of both, such as putting a rhyming refrain into a prose work – but make sure to keep these simple and easy to remember otherwise you risk confusing very young readers. For an even simpler way of making children play, use onomatopoeia – encouraging readers to repeat the sounds they hear in the story, from the growls of a monster to the moos of a cow.

SECRET CLUB

There are also more complex methods of ensuring that your book is interactive. One is to theme the book around one big riddle or question, giving the readers plenty of opportunity to guess the answer. An excellent example of this is *Where's Spot?* by Eric Hill, which used flaps on each page to cover the title character, but gimmicks like this aren't by any means essential. Joan L. Nodset's *Who Stole the*

Farmer's Hat? has readers hunting down the missing item and attempting to predict the next event, an activity that encourages them to read the book again and again.

One of the best ways to create a sense of playfulness in your book is to reawaken the child within. Take a trip in IDEA 8, *The golden years.*

Try another idea…

An interesting spin on this is to let readers in on the secret even when the characters are in the dark. They will shout out the answer and revel in the excitement of knowing something that the characters in the book do not. If you're feeling brave, or experimental, then there is also the option of breaking down the 'fourth wall' – to use theatre parlance – between the reader and the book. This means that characters interact directly with readers, addressing the children and asking them questions. Combined with the previous technique, this approach can provide endless fun.

NEVER-ENDING STORY

Getting your young readers to talk about the book after they've read it is another great way to encourage interaction, and an easy way to achieve this is to leave the book open-ended. Invite readers to continue the creative thread of the tale, encourage them to imagine what happens after the last page. Don't simply cut off the story mid-way through – a practice as infuriating for children as it is for adults. Instead, try to create a circular tale where the ending resembles the beginning, promising a new adventure that readers can imagine and talk about themselves.

'You can discover more about a person in an hour of play than in a year of conversation.'
PLATO

Defining idea…

193

How did it go?

Q I'm having trouble using any of your ideas. Can I just leave it to the illustrator to encourage readers to jump in and play?

A *Hmm... I'm not sure I approve, but there's nothing wrong with this attitude. As well as the visual interaction provided by the illustrations, you can use the artwork to get kids thinking and talking about the story in new, exciting ways. Ask the illustrator to add mini-plots or activities to their illustrations – inviting the reader to count or search for various elements. Or create a sub-plot that is purely illustrative – perhaps a girl struggling with a kite in the background of every image?*

Q I've written a story that uses play, but I'm not sure if it's the sort of thing that kids will enjoy. Is there a good way of sending it out for a test run?

A *The best way to see if your idea works is to test it on any willing children – your own, those of family or friends or even neighbours (never ask children you don't know). Get some honest feedback from both children and parents – do they enjoy participating in the story, and does it become repetitive after the third reading? The most important part is the fidget test – if children look bored, shuffle, talk about other things or try and escape then you know you've a bit more work to do.*

45

Showing off

Writing is all about telling stories, but the act of telling isn't enough to engage a reader.

The first commandment of writing is always show, don't tell, and by following this divine rule you'll enable children and adults alike to project their own experience into your writing.

Which of these sounds more exciting: going to wizard school and having loads of incredible adventures, or listening to a friend giving you endless anecdotes about when he went to wizard school and had loads of incredible adventures?

Unless you have a phobia of wizards, the former will be the desirable experience, and the same rule applies to books – when reading, children don't want to be told a story, they want to feel like they are in the middle of the adventure. If you 'show' events in your writing, they are pulled in to the story; if you simply 'tell' them, they are pushed out.

Here's an idea for you...

Try and imagine your own worst nightmare or a time when you were absolutely terrified. On one sheet of paper, or a page of your notebook, *tell* a reader about it through description. Next, write about the same thing but attempt to *show* it, paying close attention to action and emotion and sensory detail. Pull out all the stops to try and convey the horror of the situation, the fear and the panic. A comparison of the two results will show you everything you need to know about which is more evocative.

ALL ABOARD

Good writing is all about transporting readers, making them forget about the words on the page and actually feel as though they are part of the action. You don't simply want to tell them that the teenage hero is fighting with an evil warlord, you want to make them sense the danger, hear the clash of swords, smell the sweat and blood of battle, feel the pain of a wound and the panic of imminent death. Children won't always believe what they're told but they will always trust their own senses, and if they are drawn into the story, into the hero's shoes, they will live the adventure as if it was their own.

When you tell a story you are simply describing what is happening. 'The jailer threw Adam into the cell, closing the door with a crunch. After locking it, he laughed menacingly then walked away.' Yawn! You're explaining events without dramatising them, preventing your readers from making any emotional connection to the hero. Your words are devoid of any humanity, any depth, so readers become detached and their minds begin to wander.

Showing an event through the senses and thoughts of your protagonist invites readers into the scene rather than telling it from afar – the character becomes real because the reader becomes the character. 'Adam felt himself shoved forwards and he tripped, falling onto the hard floor of the cell. He clambered to his feet, and through the tears that were filling his eyes he saw the jailer's twisted sneer as the door slammed shut.'

THE OUTER LIMITS

If you simply tell a story, you're assuming that children need things spelled out in minute detail, and you're not asking them to contribute to the experience. They have incredible imaginations, so don't feel like you have to explain everything in a scene. Show the key details, the emotions and the action, and credit your readers with enough creative power to fill in the blanks. This way they will bring part of their own life to the text, projecting their own experience into the story – essentially it becomes a story for them rather than one that is simply told to them.

Of course, showing things is considerably harder than just telling them. You have to push your imagination to its limits in order to show things in a way that is moving, exciting and above all believable. The key is to immerse yourself in your own story – not just to see it happening but to live it out inside your head. Focus on the action, emotion, dialogue and the five senses, and use specific details in your work. Don't just write that a character is afraid, think about how you feel when you are scared and transfer these feelings to your characters. Only by showing, not telling, will they truly seem alive.

Telling instead of showing is one of the great sins of writing, but there are six more you should know about. Get to know your demons in IDEA 47, *Cardinal sins*.

Try another idea...

'Don't say the old lady screamed – bring her on and let her scream.'
MARK TWAIN

Defining idea...

How did it go?

Q I've been showing everything and my book is now 3,000 pages long! Is it always better to show than to tell?

A   As always, there are exceptions to the rule. Of course you don't want to show everything in a piece of writing – nobody wants to see every part of every scene in minute detail. Many new writers make the mistake of showing absolutely everything in their work. They describe a character's every action – boiling the kettle, putting a teabag into the cup and so on. Only show the things that are essential to the plot, and feel free to tell anything that is just necessary to move the story along.

Q Hmm... I'm still not really sure when to show and when to tell. Is there a foolproof way to know?

A   There is, but unfortunately it's not until you've finished writing. From personal experience it's usually easier to work out where you should have shown and not told, and vice versa, when you're editing. As you read through your work, look out for moments when something about the narrative causes you to suddenly become aware of the writing, not the events of the story. This usually happens when you have been telling instead of showing, but it can also be when you've shown too much. Rewriting the section using the method you didn't try before – either showing or telling – usually helps fix the problem.

46

Nip / Tuck

There are two sides to every writer's brain: the creative side, which wants to unleash its imagination, and the editor, the control freak who wants to complain about everything.

Be successful by getting these opposites to work together.

The problem is that the internal editor is either never given access to your work at all, or is let in at the worst possible time – when your creative side is in the process of writing something wonderful. But, like all great mortal enemies, it's essential that you keep the two sides of your brain as far apart as possible (not literally...).

TIME SHARE

When you're writing, it's essential that you let your creative side have as much freedom as possible. This unrestrained creative output is the raw material, the essence of your work, and if you pause after every sentence to check for typos and grammatical errors then your creative flow is just going to keep stalling and eventually just stop. When writing a first draft forget about your editor and just write.

Here's an idea for you...

Learn to ignore your internal editor when you're writing. When you've finished the whole thing, it's always best to put it away and let it rest for a while, anything from a few days to six months. You'll still be too engaged with it to notice its flaws – you need to see it from a distance, as if you were reading a book by a stranger. Each time you edit leave the book for a few days before reading it again, and always check it against the original to see which is better.

Of course your editor has to come out and inspect things sooner or later. But you should only start editing your writing when your creative side has stopped work. The creative side of your brain will claim to have written a perfect piece of writing, but don't be fooled – your first draft will be full of things that would make a publisher weep (and not in a good way). Trust your internal editor to read through and make changes.

STRUCTURAL ENGINEERS

It's often a good idea to read through every chapter once you've finished it, but the main edit is going to come when you've finished your entire book. The most important thing that your internal editor needs to check for is structural faults – any place where the pace of the book seems unbearably slow or ridiculously fast. Read through and ask yourself honestly if the beginning truly grabs you, if the middle sags a little or if the ending is unsatisfying.

Let your editor uncap a red pen and go to work. If the beginning of your book drags on then maybe you need to cut your first chapter, or condense the first few chapters to liven up the pace. If the middle loses momentum then think about any new areas of conflict you could expose your heroes to, challenges or setbacks that can up the tension a notch. If the climax of your book is a disappointment, then you probably need to write the final scenes again, making it more dramatic and raising the stakes for your characters.

Give your red pen a good workout in IDEA 47, *Cardinal sins*.

Try another idea...

Be brave, and don't be afraid to change things even if they're integral to the plot. It may feel strange carving up writing that you've dedicated so much time and energy to, but these edits might turn a mediocre piece of work into something amazing. This is your sandbox time, this is where you get to play and try out new things, so don't be shy! Just always, *always* keep a copy of the original, because there's nothing worse than deciding your changes suck but realising you've been working on your only copy.

SPIT AND POLISH

Once your internal editor has worked on the structure of your book, read through again to look for any language and style problems. You may not think you know what to look for but believe me, you do – anything about your writing that makes you squirm or cringe a little. Never ignore this feeling. Clichés, abstractions, outdated and unrealistic language, obscurity, lecturing, vague description, clumsy dialogue, lazy characterisation, condescension and just plain old waffle – these will all make you squirm because they are all examples of bad writing. Let your editor cut the chaff, then call on your creative side again to make some improvements.

'The beautiful part of writing is that you don't have to get it right the first time, unlike, say, a brain surgeon.'
ROBERT CORMIER, US author

Defining idea...

How did
it go?

Q I can't stop listening to my internal editor when I'm writing and it's ruining my creative flow. What can I do?

A *Try and get to know your internal editor as intimately as possible. The better you can predict what will be criticised, the easier it is to ignore what's being said – eventually you'll be able to tune it out.*

Q My internal editor is cutting everything. How do I know when to stop?

A *There's no easy way to know when a piece of work is finished, you'll just, well, know! If you think you might have lost the plot, so to speak, step away from the manuscript for a few more days or weeks and your critical faculties should reappear.*

Q I can't wait all that time! What if I get hit by a bus in three weeks and it's still resting under my bed?

A *It's great to meet somebody as paranoid as me! If you really can't wait, then there are other ways to distance yourself. Read it aloud, or have somebody read it to you, or record yourself and play it back. It's surprising how different your words will sound when they enter through the ears instead of the eyes; you'll know instantly when you hear something you don't like. Or give it to somebody to read – make sure it's somebody you can trust, but who isn't too close to you. If you get feedback, don't ignore it, even if it's not what you wanted to hear.*

47

Cardinal sins

You've finished your novel, congratulations! So why the long face?

If you've completed a piece of work, maybe even just a chapter, and it's lacking that certain something, you may be guilty of one of writing's seven cardinal sins.

Almost all manuscripts that fail to impress an editor show evidence of one of these sins, and if your writing isn't working the way you want it to, then one of the best ways to fix it is to identify which sin it is. Don't worry, you won't get flayed by a bunch of priests for committing these sins of children's writing – all writers have made the same mistakes – but correcting them could vastly improve your book's chances of reaching the heavenly bookshelves, not the hellish slush pile.

THE FINAL COUNTDOWN

I'll start with number seven and work my way to the top. This is having no clear point-of-view character. Children like to relate to a single, clearly identified person in a story – somebody they will root for and empathise with. If it isn't clear right

Here's an idea for you... If you've finished a piece of writing then go through it looking for any of the cardinal sins. Get seven different coloured pens to mark your manuscript – one for each. This way a quick glance at any reoccurring colours will let you see anything you are particularly guilty of. When you've marked them, think about ways you can remedy the problem. Even if you've only finished one chapter, try this exercise – it's better to spot any bad habits now than have to edit them out later.

from the start whose story is being told, readers will grow disinterested. Unlike adult books, children's stories usually only have one such character, although if you do use multiple viewpoints make sure one – generally a kid – always takes priority.

Number six: Are you telling instead of showing? If your writing doesn't have much of a punch then the chances are there is too much straight narrative (known in the trade as 'telling') and not enough action and dialogue ('showing'). If there is, then the story is at risk of sounding like a summary. Children want to feel like they're there, in the heat of the action and in fear for their lives, and this can only be done by showing. Try converting some of the narrative into action and dialogue.

GETTING CLOSER

Cardinal sin numero five is an easier one to identify: the overuse of unnecessary words. New writers are often guilty of going crazy with adjectives, adverbs and other chaff, especially when it comes to picture books. Because so much can be shown in illustrations, there is often no need for it. You don't have to say 'her favourite red hat', for example, because the picture shows the colour. Novelists are just as guilty – there is no need to say 'he shouted loudly' or 'she nodded her head'. Unwanted verbiage like this will make an editor shudder.

Speech is the focus for the fourth sin. If your dialogue doesn't sound real then your characters will appear artificial. Children don't talk like adults in real life, so if they sound too formal in your writing your readers will know they're fake. Take a close look at your dialogue and ask yourself if it's realistic. And make sure it's punctuated correctly!

You've also got to make sure your manuscript looks immaculate before it's sent to a publisher. Get some presentation tips in IDEA 48, *Play by the rules.*

Try another idea...

THE TOP THREE

In third place is the absence of a narrative hook – the opening sentence or page which grips readers and makes them want to read on. If it's not there, your readers will grow bored after the first few lines and move on to something else. First impressions are everything with kids' books, so make sure yours packs a punch.

Number two is a short one, but easy to fix. There's nothing children hate more than an adult who arrives to save the day. Of course it happens all the time in real life, that's what parents are for, but readers need to see a character their own age (or close to it) solving problems. It empowers them.

'I can't write five words but that I change seven.'
DOROTHY PARKER

Defining idea...

The worst sin a new writer can make, however, the one that will guarantee a rejection slip, is... an absence of conflict. Good plots are all about problems, and the way characters overcome them. If there are no problems, then characters face no challenges or struggles and probably just bumble around twiddling their thumbs. Your character has to face conflict – problems that grow increasingly worse throughout the book – only resolving them at the end. Without conflict there is no story.

Q **Are there any other things I should look out for when I'm editing? There must be sins that aren't cardinal!**

How did it go?

A *Yup, look out for the 'cardigan sins' – the ones that appear harmless but are still criminal. Examples of these are anything which is unnecessary, which slows down the pace and makes the book difficult to read. If you're not sure about a scene, ask yourself if it contributes anything to the plot. If there's a character you are doubtful about then ask yourself if that person needs to be included at all.*

Q **I'm worried that all this revision will remove the individuality from my work. These words are precious, and the more I lose the less the work feels like it's mine. Can you help?**

A *Well, the truth is that revision is actually all about making your work more personal because the idea is that you're removing all the clichés, repetitions, adverbs, adjectives and so on that anybody could have written. One of the reasons bad writing is bad is because it's so predictable, because it's easy and because lazy writers resort to it all the time. By stripping every last poorly written word from your book you're making it more personal, and more unique.*

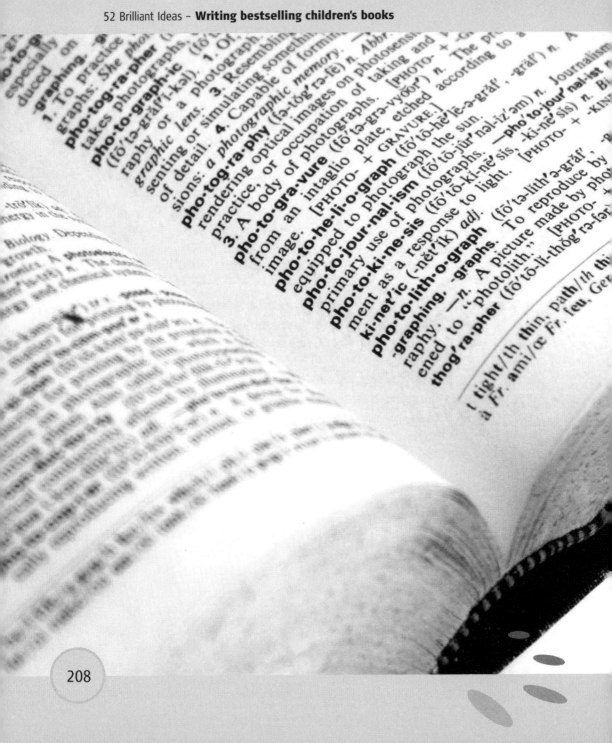

48

Play by the rules

Ask yourself, if you were going to meet a publisher would you dress in a ripped shirt, red Wellington boots and a polka-dot bikini? Hopefully, the answer is no.

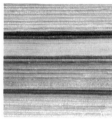

So think twice before sending a manuscript that's either full of gimmicks or so battered that it looks like it's passed through an elephant's digestive system.

Editors and agents are very busy. They see hundreds of manuscripts a month and if yours arrives in a tatty bundle that explodes all over the floor as soon as it's out of the envelope then it's probably going straight back in the post – or the recycling bin. First impressions are everything, so make sure your manuscript shines.

FINE TUNING

It may seem like a bit of a no-brainer, but the first thing you should do is check your spelling, grammar and punctuation. I was in such a hurry to send off *The Inventors* that I just stuffed the whole thing in an envelope without page numbers or even a proper edit, and it was only a few weeks afterwards when I was reading it

Here's an idea for you...

Set up a template on your word processor now, creating a large margin on the left and plenty of space on the other sides. It means you have to spend less time fidgeting with layout when you're finally ready to submit your book. Don't try typing with double-spacing, though, as it can be distracting.

through that I realised just how many typos I'd left in. Copyediting is expensive, and editors often favour manuscripts that need little or no work, so use a spellchecker carefully and invest in a guide to grammar.

DRESSED FOR CHURCH

It's also important to set out your work as cleanly and clearly as possible on the page. Leave a large (say four-centimetre) margin on the left hand side and plenty of space on the other margins, which makes your work much more pleasant to read. Stick to a plain font in size twelve, always in black and always double-spaced. Indent the first line of every paragraph except for the first one of each chapter, don't leave extra lines between paragraphs and never forget to number the pages continuously.

When you've perfected the layout, print your work out on good-quality, clean, white A4 paper – thick enough to withstand a great deal of thumbing. Only print on one side of the paper, and make sure every line is legible. If you're sending a picture book dummy, then make sure your text is printed clearly on the page. Never bind your work with a hole punch or staples – it should be left loose, kept in order with a couple of elastic bands.

Resist any temptation to experiment with gimmicks and presentation tricks. These won't woo, they'll just irritate. If you're writing a story about a toy car that comes to life, don't send your manuscript inside a toy car. By all means suggest ways your book can be marketed, but all editors want to do at this stage is see how good a writer you are, and in order to do that they need to be able to read your manuscript easily.

Send your work to a publisher and wait for your dreams to come true. See how in IDEA 49, *Hook, line and sinker.*

Try another idea...

MARK YOUR TERRITORY

Make sure that an editor knows the manuscript is yours. As a publisher as well as a writer, I know what an editor's desk looks like – a mountain of papers all spilling into each other. On the title page, write the title of the piece and your name in the centre, and note your address, telephone number, email and the number of pages submitted in one corner. It's also worth adding a header on each page with the name of the piece and your surname, or writing your name, telephone number and the title of the piece on the back of each page so that the publisher knows how to contact you if they get separated from the title page (a common occurrence).

'You must keep sending work out; you must never let a manuscript do nothing but eat its own head off in a drawer.'
ISAAC ASIMOV

Defining idea...

Always remember that this is your work, and if it doesn't look like you care about it or treat it with respect then an editor may assume you're not that bothered. Give the impression that you're sending something valuable and publishers will always pay it more attention.

'Manuscript: something submitted in haste and returned at leisure.'
OLIVER HERFORD

Defining idea...

How did it go?

Q   I could lay my text out like a proper book. That's sure to impress a publisher because it means they've got less to do! Right?

A   *Wrong! As a publisher, it always baffles me when people send in manuscripts in a Word document which has reduced in size to resemble a page, and claim in their cover letters that they've already typeset the book. They haven't, they've usually just set out the text in a way that makes it more difficult for an editor to read. When a book is typeset the text will be stripped from the original document and entered into a completely new piece of software. It's always best just to send your work on standard A4 paper because this is what editors find easiest. The exception is if you're sending a picture book dummy, when it's acceptable to lay out your text and any doodles as they will appear on the finished book.*

Q   Is there anything else I should know before sending my work out?

A   *Never, ever send your only copy. It sounds like the stupidest piece of advice in the world, but I know people who've done it then realised with horror that it's been lost in the post or misplaced at the publishers. Always burn a few copies onto CDs, give them to trusted people in case your house burns down, and print out a second paper copy so that, even if the world's technology rebels, you'll still possess your book.*

49

Hook, line and sinker

You've finished your book, there isn't a word out of place, the characters are practically leaping from the page and the plot is perfect.

So stop staring at it and find a publisher — the children of the world want to know your name!

One of the hardest things about writing is learning to let it go, releasing it to the outside world where it must fend for itself. But have faith that all your hard work has paid off; your book has evolved from the tiniest seed of an idea into something wonderful. It is sure to make friends in the outside world – providing you send it to the right places.

GOING SOLO

The vast majority of new writers approach publishers on their own – in other words without an agent. But think carefully about who you make contact with. Don't send your manuscript off to Aardvark and Sons Academic Publishers just because they're the first name in the book.

*Here's an
idea for
you...*

Don't leave a synopsis until the last minute. As soon as you know what your book will be about, try and sum it up in a page. Don't just describe what happens, keep your writing fast-paced, dynamic and exciting and try and capture the essence of your story in this short space; think of it like a film trailer. It's also useful to write a longer synopsis which describes the story in a little more detail – just in case an editor wants further information.

Spend a day doing a little research. Find out which publishers or imprints (a section of a larger publishing house) are most likely to respond well. The best way to do this is to visit a bookshop or library and find titles similar to the one you've just written. Note down the name of relevant publishers, then order a copy of their catalogues or take a look at their websites to see their full range of titles. Alternatively, buy a copy of the *Children's Writers' and Artists' Yearbook.* A little research will also help you check whether their authors are mainly first-timers or seasoned professionals. If it looks like your book would sit nicely alongside their other titles, then send it to one of them.

WHO'S WHO?

When you've decided which publisher to approach, you should also devote a little time to checking submissions procedure, most importantly whether the company is currently accepting new work. A quick glance at the website should let you know what they expect to see – usually a cover letter, a synopsis and the first few chapters (if the word count of the book is under 8,000 they'll probably want to see the whole thing). If in doubt, then ring and enquire about exactly what you should send. *Don't* ask to speak to an editor – the receptionist can help you.

Most importantly, find out the name of the editor you need to send your submission to – a 'Dear Madam' or, worse, 'Dear Sir' (the majority of people in the business are women) will rankle. Five minutes looking for the right contact will mean your manuscript is much more warmly received.

COVER ME!

The synopsis of your work is an important tool when you're looking for a publisher. No editor has the time to read every manuscript that comes in, so you should send a short description of what the book's about. This shouldn't be a dreary summary, but an exciting piece of between 300 and 1,000 words which sums up the story. It should also briefly describe the genre, format and age group of the book, as well as offer a hint to its theme. Most importantly, try and let a publisher know the book's 'hook' – the commercially appealing factor which will instantly let an editor know that the title will sell.

Lastly, include a cover letter. This is a short introduction to your book and yourself, written in a simple and professional way – it's a business document. Be brief and to the point. Never write pages about your life history (unless you've already been published, or it's directly relevant to the book, in which case make a brief note) and never tell a publisher your kids loved the book. Keep everything to three or four paragraphs, and make sure your grammar and spelling are immaculate.

With any luck, an editor will write back and ask to see the rest of your manuscript but don't despair if you get a rejection – just try again. What isn't right for one may be solid gold to another.

> Rejection can be a horrible thing, but it's part of every writer's education. Don't despair, read IDEA 52, *It's all about you.*

Try another idea...

> **'Advice from this elderly practitioner is to forget publishers and just roll a sheet of copy paper into your machine and get lost in your subject.'**
> E. B. WHITE

Defining idea...

How did
it go?

Q   Wow, a publisher has accepted my manuscript, it's going to be published! Quick, give me a pen so I can sign the contract! Right?

A   *Hold your horses! First, congratulations, it's a success well earned. Second, never sign anything before you understand and are happy with every word. The euphoria of getting a deal will often mean you couldn't care less about the small print. Always get someone to read through the contract and give you some honest advice. You'd need a whole book to go through contract technicalities, but a good solicitor can help. Or, even better, if you're a member of the Society of Authors they'll give you free contractual advice. Believe me, it's essential to get help – you may find you've signed away your soul.*

Q   So, is it worth getting an agent?

A   *Some successful writers have one, some choose not to. It's down to whether you think you can find a publisher yourself and handle your own financial affairs when you do. Agents take 10–25% of your basic commission, but will force editors to read your work and make sure you get the best deal possible – a very fair transaction. The most important thing about having an agent is that it frees you to do what you love: write.*

50

On the bandwagon

The success of a children's book really is 1% inspiration and 99% perspiration – and that perspiration comes from marketing and publicity.

This doesn't mean dressing up in a dinosaur suit and handing out flyers, but if you market your book with passion and inventiveness then it will be a success.

A great many writers think that as soon as a publisher has said yes then it's time to put your feet up. All publishers, especially the big ones, will organise their own marketing – which ranges from a few leaflets to covering Big Ben with a giant poster of the front cover. But doing your own bit to spread the word can give your book a huge boost. Your book needs you behind it.

KITTED OUT

The best place to start is a simple press kit containing snappy but exciting information about both you and your book. It should include a brief synopsis (and the age it is aimed at), a writing résumé of past titles or other related work, such as

Here's an
idea for
you...

Even if you haven't finished your book yet – even if you haven't started – get yourself a folder and write MARKETING on it. Write down any ideas you have for promoting your book, and make a note of any contacts you can send a press pack or review copy to when it is published. Every time you get a marketing idea, put it in there. Add useful information, and by the time you come to publish your book your folder will be bursting with ways to promote it.

teaching and your publisher's author schedule (if you have one). Most importantly, it needs a 500-word biography which details your inspirations or experiences and possibly a funny anecdote or piece of information about the book.

This is a chance to showcase yourself, so make sure it looks impressive. Keep everything simple – print it out on heavy white paper in a clear, black font and include a picture of you and a copy of your book jacket. Send the kit off to newspapers and magazines, booksellers, teachers – anybody you think might be interested – including a cover letter (personally addressed). Explain that you are hoping to promote your book through the media and through readings in schools and bookshops. It may seem like a lot of effort, but the exposure it creates will make it worthwhile.

SPREAD THE WORD

Good promotion is about letting as many people know about your book as possible, and making them want to read it. When it is out, send copies to reviewers (even if only one out of twenty is reviewed it will generate many more readers) and authors or celebrities who can endorse your work. Get in touch with radio stations and television production companies. Local shows will often be very willing to showcase regional talent, and if you tie in your book with a current event or relevant topic then you may even get on national programmes.

Read IDEA 51, *The front line*, and learn how to make the most from going back to school.

Try another idea...

BLOOD FROM A STONE

If your publisher is willing to fork out a bit of marketing cash (if they are too tight you could always dig into your own pockets if necessary) then try putting together your own fun activity pack that you can give away to your readers. When *The Inventors* was published I made up Inventing Packs with notebooks, pencils, a mug and a T-shirt, all with the book's logo on. I paid for these myself (it was cheaper than it sounds), but because I could give them away as prizes it led to a great deal of interest from children's magazines and shows.

Think about whether an activity pack would help promote your book, and if so what items would best reflect its theme. Check out printing companies, get some quotes then approach your publisher – who will be much more willing to pay if there's an exact cost rather than a guesstimate.

'There is no such thing as bad publicity except your own obituary.'
BRENDAN BEHAN

Defining idea...

CAUGHT IN THE WEB

Last, but definitely not least, get yourself a website. Pretty much all children these days use computers, and most check on their favourite authors. If you have a personal, fun site with information, a regularly updated blog (online diary), photos, details about when you are appearing in public (readings, not just popping to a shop) and preferably some interactive games or activities (including competitions), then you're helping to create the idea of an *author* in the minds of your readers, not just a book. It's the beginning of a fan base.

Q **So, you can spend half an hour every six months marketing your book, right?**

How did it go?

A *You can if you don't want anybody to know about it. Get into the habit of spending fifteen minutes every day thinking about ways to promote it – whether or not it has been published. You'll soon get used to thinking originally about marketing, and the exposure it will eventually generate will be instrumental to your book's success. If your book hasn't been accepted yet, then proof that you've committed so much time to marketing already will certainly make a publisher inclined to take you on.*

Q **Any tips on shameless self-promotion?**

A *If you're not worried about blowing your own trumpet then hold a book party for yourself when your book's out. Match the theme to the subject – if it's a pirate novel, for example, make it fancy dress – and invite journalists, booksellers, teachers, reviewers and anybody else who might be useful (don't forget friends and family, they might be miffed if their invitations go missing). This can be a great way to get people talking.*

Q **I'm trying to fill my Marketing folder but it's barer than Mother Hubbard's cupboards at the moment. Any hints?**

A *Writing may be a one-person show but publicity isn't. Recruit friends, family and coworkers, use and abuse them for ideas about how best to promote your book. If you don't know anyone useful the chances are somebody else will.*

51

The front line

Writing is often a solitary venture where the only company you have is a bored cat and a chocolate biscuit. But when your book is published all this must change.

Standing in front of a classroom full of young readers can be scarier than charging into battle at Helm's Deep, but it's vital if you want to build up an audience.

Have you ever thought about going back to school? First school, that is. School visits can be a great way to supplement your income during the early days of writing, but they can also start a chain reaction, making your book the most talked about in town.

Writing a book for children is one thing, but public readings are something else entirely. There's something very safe about sitting at a desk by yourself scribbling, and the thought of performing your work in front of a class full of children can be terrifying. One wrong move, after all, and you'll have a riot on your hands. Right?

Here's an idea for you...

Even if you haven't finished yet, start to think about how you could present your book to a class. Come up with a short presentation, followed by a programme of activities that could last for an hour. Think of creative games and exercises that will get children excited about the content of your book, and if possible try them out on kids you know. Publishers love an author who's prepared!

Wrong! Authors who are nervous about doing readings in schools only have to remember one thing: having you in the classroom is a treat, it means the kids get an exciting break from work. For this reason, school visits can be great fun, connecting you with your audience and even becoming the most rewarding aspect of being a published author.

QUITE A PERFORMANCE

But before you even think about getting in touch with a school, plan out your presentation. *Presentation?* Yes, reading in schools doesn't just involve reading – kids don't want to just sit and listen to you dictate a chapter of your book. No matter how good the book is, they want to feel like they are being involved. And teachers will expect your visit to have some kind of interactive, educational benefit.

When I go into schools to promote *The Inventors*, I start by asking the kids what their favourite inventions are. Classrooms are usually quiet to begin with, so I encourage them to think back two hundred years and try and imagine how living then would be different to living now. I ask which inventions have most changed the world since then – computers, cars, the toilet. At some point I usually read a very short extract from the book, then I get the kids to think of their own inventions which they draw or describe in a short story. By the end they're usually frantically sketching machines and chattering excitedly to themselves about being inventors.

Look at IDEA 50, *On the bandwagon*, for some other ways to sell yourself to your public.

Try another idea...

GET CREATIVE

Try and work out how you could do a presentation around your book. Find the hook and use it to design some activities that will help kids get excited about the story. Activities that you can suggest include question and answer sessions – but never put anyone on the spot – brainstorming, writing or illustrating exercises and even having students act out a story.

Another angle to take is to focus on the aspect of writing itself. Talk to the children about creating new worlds and people, about how you got started, about where you get your ideas. Include any hilarious anecdotes from the process (don't be afraid to elaborate for comic effect). If you're worried about attentions wavering, then incorporate visuals into your presentation – slides of interesting photos, or objects that have inspired you or that you've included in your story.

'The mediocre teacher tells. The good teacher explains. The superior teacher demonstrates. The great teacher inspires.'
WILLIAM ARTHUR WARD, US author

Defining idea...

GETTING IN

Once you've created a presentation, start approaching local schools. If your children, grandchildren, nieces and nephews and so on are at school, volunteer to talk to their classes – it's a great way of getting the ball rolling. Write to headteachers or librarians at other schools, describing yourself and your book, and giving an outline of your presentation and what it offers children. Sell yourself! Most schools are extremely receptive to authors coming in to give talks – just make sure that the class you are visiting is the right age group for your book.

Q I've tried my presentation on some kids and they said it was boring. What am I missing?

A Maybe you're not excited enough. A successful school visit isn't just about making the kids have fun – you have to enjoy yourself too. If you're wildly excited about the presentation, and the book, then it will be contagious – guaranteed. Try and incorporate more audience participation, and make sure that you're visiting the right age group. Don't be afraid to ask your audience what would have made the talk more fun, and change your presentation accordingly.

Q I remember what we used to do to supply teachers when I was a kid. What if I lose control and get the same treatment?

A Make sure the teacher stays in the classroom, and avoid any obvious jokes by making them yourself. If someone is trying to show off, focus on that child. Never look flustered or embarrassed – kids can smell weakness and it will only make things worse. Just laugh it off and they will laugh with you, not at you.

Q What about money?

A At first you'll probably be volunteering. When you're more established then make sure you settle a fee in advance and sign a contract that stipulates what you'll be doing, when and for how long. If there is no contract, make one yourself – it just prevents any painful misunderstandings (there are plenty of samples online).

How did it go?

It's all about you

If I could recommend one guideline to always follow when writing then it would be this: what makes your writing unique and powerful, what really appeals to children, is you.

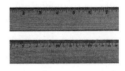

So always stay true to yourself and trust your instincts when putting pen to paper.

It's tempting to look at the sheer wealth of books and resources that exist on creative writing for children and think that somebody has a foolproof formula you can follow for success. The truth is, however, that creative writing has no real rules. There are guidelines, there are hints and tips, there are suggestions and exercises and examples and warnings. But ultimately you must write to the beat of your own heart.

LEARN TO FORGET

The best way to treat any guide to creative writing is to learn the rules and then forget them. Don't start whacking yourself over the head with a sledgehammer until you've knocked out all the relevant memories – all this means is that you can't rely on guidelines alone to produce a good piece of writing.

Here's an idea for you...

Never lose that sense of play – not just when thinking of ideas but when writing as well. Be courageous, don't be afraid to try new things, to be different. If it doesn't work then just throw it away and try something else. If it does work you'll end up with something wonderful, and publishers will beat a path to your door. Above all, keep a spirit of adventure – if you can lose yourself in your imagination, then so can the world.

These ideas and suggestions are designed to help you look at the world differently, to allow you to pluck ideas out of the air and lay them down on the page in a way that makes your writing addictive. They will help you look deep inside yourself, freeing the inner child and letting it fuel the sense of adventure and fun in your work. And they will help you learn how to take the mass of feeling and emotion and drama that drives your imagination and shape it into a wonderful, coherent narrative.

PAINTING BY NUMBERS

It isn't like painting by numbers, and you can't expect to follow a few set prescriptions and end up with a work of pure genius. To create a book that has the power to engage and excite children all over the world, you need to walk your own path – to produce something that resonates with your own personality, your own sense of adventure and intrigue. Don't lose sight of what you've learned, but see the guidelines as a way to free your creativity, not restrain it – a way to channel your energy onto the page.

KEEP YOUR CHIN UP

It's worth saying a little something here about rejection. No matter how good your writing is, there will always be editors who decide it's not for them. Pretty much every successful writer has been rejected – the most famous example being J. K. Rowling, whose *Harry Potter* books were deemed unworthy by twelve publishing houses (all of which will probably kick themselves for ever) before they were taken on.

If you think you might have writer's block, use the same tactics to quash it as you used with that other mythical beast, the blank page. Ride into battle in IDEA 4, *Starting off*.

Try another idea...

If you receive a rejection slip, then don't despair. If you've written from the heart then persevere and you will be successful. Whatever you do, don't try and change your writing because you think that's what a publisher wants. It's fine to take advice, and make a few changes here and there, but never give up the spirit that makes it yours. Write a book that's true to you, tell the story you want to tell with the passion that it deserves, and sooner or later an editor will fall in love with it.

'As a writer you are free. You are about the freest person that ever was.'
URSULA LE GUIN

Defining idea...

GORDY'S FINAL THOUGHT

The only reason to write is because you love writing, and because you want to share the adventure. If you write to make money, or write for fame, then your writing won't come from the heart, it won't be truly yours and any child who starts to read will know that straight away. Creative writing must always be the most personal of subjects, it must come from your very soul. Only when it does will your work truly be embraced by children and adults, only then will it fuel the imagination of countless generations and develop the minds of the future, only then will your work be powerful, and only then will people love you for it.

Q **Aaaaargh! I've contracted writer's block. I'm never going to be able to write again. Can you help?**

How did it go?

A *Every writer knows what it's like to sit at your desk trying to write but not knowing what to say, or knowing what you want to say but being somehow powerless to say it. Writer's block always seems much worse than it actually is, and can be beaten with a mere scribble. It usually comes when you're not listening to your inner passions and beliefs, when you're not using your emotions, your physical drives, your imagination. Open a fresh page of your notebook and start something else. It doesn't matter what, just immerse yourself in your imagination and write what you see there. The more you write, the quicker the blockage will shift. When the words start flowing again, return to your story.*

Q **The block still hasn't shifted, it's got my brain and it won't give it back. Are there any more battle tips?**

A *You're probably being too negative about your capacity as a writer. All writers are plagued by negative thoughts. The chances are that most of these doubts lie deep within your unconscious, so if you ignore them or remain unaware of them they'll keep emerging again and again. Try and get them on paper, because writing them down rids them of their power – when your fears exist as words you've got control.*

The end...

Or is it a new beginning?

We hope that the ideas in this book will have inspired you to try some new things. You should be well on your way to a more creative, inspired you, brimming with ideas and inventive ambition. Perhaps you've already tried a few new things in your stories and met with a positive reaction from some young readers.

So why not let *us* know all about it? Tell us how you got on. What did it for you – what helped you beat that blank page with words that sparkle like fairy dust? Maybe you've got some tips of your own you want to share (see next page if so). And if you liked this book you may find we have even more brilliant ideas that could change other areas of your life for the better.

You'll find the Infinite Ideas crew waiting for you online at www.infideas.com.

Or if you prefer to write, then send your letters to:
Writing bestselling children's books
The Infinite Ideas Company Ltd
36 St Giles, Oxford OX1 3LD, United Kingdom

We want to know what you think, because we're all working on making our lives better too. Give us your feedback and you could win a copy of another *52 Brilliant Ideas* book of your choice. Or maybe get a crack at writing your own.

Good luck. Be brilliant.

Offer one

CASH IN YOUR IDEAS

We hope you enjoy this book. We hope it inspires, amuses, educates and entertains you. But we don't assume that you're a novice, or that this is the first book that you've bought on the subject. You've got ideas of your own. Maybe our author has missed an idea that you use successfully. If so, why not send it to yourauthormissedatrick@infideas.com, and if we like it we'll post it on our bulletin board. Better still, if your idea makes it into print we'll send you four books of your choice or the cash equivalent. You'll be fully credited so that everyone knows you've had another Brilliant Idea.

Offer two

HOW COULD YOU REFUSE?

Amazing discounts on bulk quantities of Infinite Ideas books are available to corporations, professional associations and other organisations.

For details call us on:
+44 (0)1865 514888
Fax: +44 (0)1865 514777
or e-mail: info@infideas.com

Where it's at...

brilliant ideas

Writing bestselling children's books is published by Infinite Ideas, publishers of the acclaimed **52 Brilliant Ideas** series. With the **52 Brilliant Ideas** series you can enhance your existing skills or knowledge with negligible investment of time and money and can substantially improve your performance or know-how of a subject over the course of a year. Or day. Or month. The choice is yours. There are over 45 titles published in subject areas as diverse as: Health & relationships; Sports, hobbies & games; Lifestyle & leisure and Careers, finance & personal development. To learn more, to join our mailing list or to find out about discounts and special offers visit www.infideas.com, or e-mail info@infideas.com.

The Writers' Workshop: Run by writers for writers

So you've written your brilliant children's book. What next? Agents accept only about 1 manuscript in every 1000 they receive, and only the best of the best will ever be published. With the help of *Writing bestselling children's books* and this exclusive offer from The Writers' Workshop, though, you'll be well on your way (see below for details).

The Writers' Workshop is Britain's premier editorial and advisory service for first time writers. The Writers' Workshop believes passionately that good writers have a right to high quality feedback and support – the sort that literary agents can't or won't provide.

The Writers' Workshop will read your manuscript in depth, and offer comprehensive, honest and constructive advice on what's good, what's bad, and how to fix the things that need fixing. Plus, if your manuscript is good enough to publish, they'll do all they can to help you market it successfully.

All the editors are published authors of real experience and quality – with dozens of literary awards and shortlists between them. They're the first ones to admit that writing for children is a difficult game – hard work and poorly paid. But there is nothing more fulfilling than getting your first publishing deal.

And because the Writers' Workshop is run by writers for writers, they are always, always on your side.

For more information visit www.writersworkshop.co.uk or email info@writersworkshop.co.uk.

Inspiring writers' discount

The Writers' Workshop is delighted to offer **£50 off** your first full length manuscript appraisal. For shorter work (short stories, short fiction, picture books, etc) get **10% off** their normal prices.

In order to qualify for the special discounted prices, simply remember to quote *'Writing bestselling children's books'* when contacting the Writers' Workshop or when submitting work. The number to ring is **01869 347040** or email info@writersworkshop. This offer is valid all the way through to 31 July 2008.

Full details on services, prices and editorial staff can be found on their website: www.writersworkshop.co.uk.

THE END